RIVER COTTAGE

GREAT ROASTS

RIVER COTTAGE
GREAT ROASTS

GELF ALDERSON

Hugh Fearnley-Whittingstall's
RIVER COTTAGE

BLOOMSBURY PUBLISHING
LONDON · OXFORD · NEW YORK · NEW DELHI · SYDNEY

Recipe notes

- All spoon measures are level unless otherwise stated:
  1 tsp = 5ml spoon; 1 tbsp = 15ml spoon.
- All herbs are fresh unless otherwise suggested.
- Use freshly ground or cracked black pepper unless
  otherwise listed.
- All veg and fruit should be washed. Choose organic
  fruit and veg if possible.
- Root veg, onions, garlic and ginger are peeled or
  scrubbed unless otherwise suggested.
- If using the zest of citrus fruit, choose unwaxed fruit.
- Please use free-range eggs, preferably organic.
- Opt for organic products wherever possible, including
  tinned pulses, coconut milk, kefir, yoghurt and cheeses.
- Oven timings are provided for both conventional and
  fan-assisted ovens. Individual ovens can deviate by
  10°C or more either way from the actual setting, so get
  to know your oven and use an oven thermometer to
  check the temperature.

Contents

Foreword

The roast is the most iconic of British food institutions, and rightly so. It's a celebratory meal that doesn't need an occasion, because it *is* an occasion – one that brings people together around the table. Studies suggest that the family meal is in decline, with the supposedly short supply of time and energy, and screens and devices pulling our attentions elsewhere. Yet passing plates and sharing stories over a shared meal brings so many benefits for our physical and mental health. Young children evolve their vocabulary in the to and fro of chatting over food, while teenagers who have regular family meals are more inclined to share their problems.

It might be a bold thing to say but I think the roasting tin (and its colourful extended family of 'ovenproof dishes') could save the day. The oven is the place to go when you want to rustle up a family meal, especially if time is tight. Get a bit of basic prep out of the way (keep it chunky!) and it's usually just a matter of bunging it all in, and letting the magic of heat take on the culinary transformation – caramelising the edges of carrots, rendering pork shoulder into luscious shreds of meat capped with a golden armour of crackling, or teasing out the natural sugars in fruit to the point where only a finishing trickle of honey is needed to create a phenomenal pudding.

Of course, roasts are not just about big slabs of meat or crisp golden potatoes – this is especially true for us at River Cottage. There's a vast array of ingredients, mostly from the plant kingdom, that rise to gastronomic heights in the hot box at the heart of our kitchens. We love to mingle them and spice them to bring out their finest qualities. It's a sure-fire way to boost the pleasure and satisfaction of our guests, and you will find the same when cooking for family and friends.

It turns out that the concept of 'roasting' is as broad as it is long, encompassing many techniques which would normally have us sweating over the hob. Ever tried frying an egg in a roasting tin? Or letting the slow heat of the oven create the creamiest, stir-free risotto? And you can happily roast a ratatouille, a curry, a chilli, or even a compote. These reinventions of stove-top classics often bring out new flavours and fun juxtapositions, even as they save you time and effort.

It's this playful combination of seasonal variety and co-opted, simplified techniques that's at the heart of this wonderful collection from our talented River Cottage Culinary Director, Gelf Alderson. He invites us to stretch the horizons of what we understand by roasting, without ever making it daunting or inaccessible. He brings genuine, from-the-heart and family recipes, and takes the classics like roast chicken to the next level, while also ensuring anyone can follow his lead.

This book is sure to inspire you to experiment in the way you use roasting as a technique. Once Gelf has got your creative culinary juices flowing with his oven eggy bread with summer berries, asparagus and spinach with roasted garlic butter, or his roast gooseberries with strawberries and mint, you'll want to go off-piste and have a play. And you'll find that roasting turns out to be a not-so-dark art that will soon have you inventing your own original oven-seared delights. Just flick through these pages and you'll be richly gifted with both inspiration and confidence – all you need to gather loved ones to your table for an unforgettable feast.

Hugh

Introduction

We're a nation that loves a roast. Every Sunday, up and down the country, family and friends congregate to honour this tradition, often centred around a table crammed full of our favourites: joints of well-roasted meats, Yorkshire puddings, cauliflower cheese, crispy roast potatoes and so on. Or, if like me, you were brought up with just veg, there'll be lots of well-prepared plant dishes – more than I can remember as a child. The Sunday roast is a tradition we should never lose; it's so much more than just a meal.

However, roasting isn't just for Sundays, Christmas and special occasions. Every day we roast things, often without realising and usually for simplicity – it doesn't get much easier than shoving something in the oven. So, as well as celebrating our favourites, I've tried to cook most of the recipes in just one tray or dish to cut down on that washing up we all hate, but love arguing about whose turn it is to do! Once you have that tray in the oven there's no standing over a hot stove. You can join the occasion rather than being hunkered down in the kitchen while everyone else is enjoying themselves, with the odd stir and occasional addition of ingredients at the last minute. It's a much more laid-back approach to making amazing food. You could call it lazy cooking… I call it good food, for busy people.

I grew up as a vegetarian, with lots of lovely veg being grown by my dad in a small plot. And I'm not talking about a big walled garden, just a square of land in the back garden of our council house. Looking back now, I realise this was a thrifty necessity, but seeing things grow and eating them directly from source taught me so much. It shaped me as a person, and as a chef. Although I enjoy an omnivorous diet now, I have many fond memories of family gatherings around tables laden with delicious veggie roasts, including the much-maligned – but quite delicious if properly made – nut roast. Try my mum's recipe on page 150 and put away images of tired old stuffing recipes with a couple of nuts thrown in. It's a staunch family favourite, still much in demand.

In this book I'm going to show you how we can roast for every occasion and every meal of the day. We start off with 'Breakfast and brunch' – simple one-tray assemblies, both savoury and fruity. Even with an oven fry-up, you can still enjoy that perfect runny egg, which for me is an absolute breakfast essential. We move on to 'Snacky things', ranging from a hearty leftovers frittata on page 42, which is perfect for a picnic, to my version of 'Twiglets' on page 58 and lots of other nibbly bits to enjoy with drinks. Then there's 'One-tray wonders' – the ultimate in low-maintenance all-in-one meals – a mix of dishes to impress and pure comfort food.

At River Cottage we love celebrating veg, so 'All about veg' is totally plant-based and bursting with all the flavours and vibrancy that the veg garden offers. The recipes in this chapter are all suitable for vegans. In 'Sunday roast', which features my favourite celebratory meat, fish and veg dishes, I guarantee you'll find a new weekend favourite to supplement your regular roasts. To accompany these, the 'Super sides' chapter that follows is packed with original ideas.

And, in my opinion, it's the sides that often make the meal. We finish off with 'Fruity numbers', showing how roasting makes great desserts less faffy. I've even snuck a foolproof custard in there – not technically a roast but so essential to the enjoyment of many oven-cooked puds!

A lot of what we do every day in the kitchens at River Cottage involves roasting beautiful seasonal veg and carefully sourced meat and fish. Even though it's a professional kitchen, we don't have a lot of fancy kit, as we rely on the magic that happens within a hot oven. In simple terms, we are using the heat of the oven to change the sugars in the food. A high heat leads to dark, rich caramel flavours, while the food retains its texture well. Charred edges and almost-burnt corners only add to the great taste – check out the ultimate River Cottage roasties on page 158. Roasting at a low heat softens ingredients and enhances their natural sweetness, especially veg. Slow-roasted peppers with courgettes, lentils and tomatoes on page 106 is a great example of this. And cooking meat low and slow gives meltingly tender, flavourful results. Slowly-does-it pork shoulder on page 143 illustrates this perfectly and has the added benefit of cooking overnight. I don't think it gets any better than cooking while you sleep!

You don't need much kit for roasting, but it is worth getting to know your oven. Every oven has its quirks and idiosyncrasies and the temperature on the dial may not be the temperature inside. I'd recommend getting an oven thermometer to keep a check on this. It can also tell you whether your oven is up to temperature before you add the food (if your oven doesn't do this for you). And please don't skip preheating the oven – this can change the cooking time completely. You may also find your oven has hot spots. If so, don't worry, just get into the habit of spinning your trays around during roasting so that dishes brown evenly.

It's worth investing in a set of good, solid metal roasting trays (small, medium and large), as well as a few shallow baking trays. Avoid anything cheap and thin, which is liable to buckle and bend with the heat of the oven. A good cast-iron casserole is a great investment, as are a few ceramic dishes in different sizes. Take care of your oven trays and tins and they might just last a lifetime. If you're worried about things sticking, line the roasting tray, pan or dish with a sheet of baking paper. And if you've really hammered a metal pan, pour in hot water and leave to soak overnight then wash it in the morning. Don't resort to using a metal scourer, as this is likely to damage the pan. And avoid putting anything with a coating, anything cast-iron, or those lovely pans which develop a nice patina over time, into the abrasive environment of the dishwasher.

If a recipe specifies a particular roasting dish (metal or ceramic, for example), it's important to follow that instruction because materials transfer heat in different ways. You can't roast a fry-up in a ceramic dish, for instance, because it protects the food from the intense heat of the oven. So a ceramic dish is great for slowly softening vegetables, but not so good if you want to crisp up bacon or brown an onion.

There's so much to love about roasting food. Because it doesn't involve adding water, the nutrients and flavours don't leach away. On the contrary, they are concentrated and intensified. Once we thought that all you could do with things like brassicas is boil or steam them, but today we know how delicious purple sprouting broccoli and cauliflower are with the right amount of char. Nowadays, there's not much I wouldn't try to roast – we've got a wonderful roasted lettuce recipe on page 81, which might surprise you. I've never roasted a cucumber, but come to think of it, those knobbly English ones would probably roast up nicely, so I might just give it a go....

1
BREAKFAST
& BRUNCH

You might not expect to find a chapter of breakfast recipes in a book about roasts, but it just goes to show how versatile the oven can be – you can even make eggy bread in it! Cooking up a big breakfast for a crowd can be tricky if you're trying to make a lot of different things. I want to get away from the idea that a weekend brunch involves using lots of pans and every ring on the hob, and back to celebrating the fact that it's the weekend.

Big breakfasts don't have to mean getting hot and bothered while you try to fry multiple eggs at once. Just get a baking tray out, fill it up, throw it in the oven and you'll be able to enjoy your morning with family or friends. When it's ready, put the tray in the middle of the table and everyone can have breakfast together. And – a huge bonus – with just one pan on the go, you're not going to have to spend long washing up.

At River Cottage, breakfast is about much more than just toast, porridge or cereal – it's a chance for us to get creative and can involve just as many textures, flavours, veg and fruits as any other meal. Whether you fancy tray-baked Crispy potatoes with bacon, tomatoes and spinach (page 20); Roast garlic mushrooms with parsley and eggs (page 16); Roast pearl barley and smoked fish kedgeree (page 24); Chorizo, eggs and onions with green herbs (page 29) or Roast plums with star anise, oats and kefir (page 38), we've got your brunch covered.

15

Roast garlic mushrooms with parsley and eggs

I love mushrooms for breakfast, especially with plenty of garlic. I'm using nice big flat mushrooms for this simple, classic combination but it works well with any variety. If you can get your hands on some wild mushrooms like chanterelles or girolles they'll take it to another level – just adjust the cooking time accordingly. And make sure you have a nice hunk of fresh crusty bread on the side to mop up any juices.

Serves 2

8 large flat mushrooms
2 garlic cloves, finely chopped
2 tbsp extra virgin olive oil
A knob of unsalted butter
A small bunch of flat-leaf parsley, leaves picked and roughly chopped
4 medium eggs
Sea salt and freshly cracked black pepper
Buttered sourdough, to serve

Preheat the oven to 220°C/210°C Fan/Gas 7.

Cut the mushrooms into 1cm thick slices. Place them in a medium baking dish with the chopped garlic and extra virgin olive oil and tumble together. (Don't be tempted to add salt at this stage as this would make the mushrooms tough.) Bake in the oven for 10 minutes.

Remove the dish from the oven, add the knob of butter and stir gently. Return to the oven for 3–5 minutes until the mushrooms are nice and soft. Take out of the oven, season with salt and pepper and toss through the parsley.

Using the back of a spoon, make 4 hollows in the baked mushrooms and crack the eggs into these. Season the eggs with salt and pepper. Place the dish back in the oven for 4–6 minutes until the whites of the eggs are just set but the yolks are still runny. Check them often to make sure the yolks don't firm up, unless that's how you like them!

Serve the mushrooms and eggs with warm sourdough... and a smile.

Swaps
Use any variety of mushrooms you like. Try replacing the parsley with chopped tarragon or snipped chives. And if you're not a fan of eggs, replace them with a ball of mozzarella – thickly sliced and cooked on top of the mushrooms until creamy and stringy.

Roast asparagus, lettuce and eggs

I grew up near Worcester in the Vale of Evesham, which is famous for its asparagus, so it's always been a really big thing for me. The key is to eat it as close to picking as possible and never resort to imported asparagus. I'm fortunate to have Joel, a close friend, who grows an acre of asparagus for me at River Cottage so I can cook it the day it is picked. It's definitely worth getting as close to the source as possible, so do a bit of 'digging around' for your asparagus to enjoy it in its all-too-short season.

Serves 2–3

2 bunches of asparagus
3 Baby Gem lettuce, halved
   lengthways
3 tbsp extra virgin olive oil
4 or 6 medium eggs
Sea salt and freshly cracked
   black pepper

Preheat the oven to 220°C/210°C Fan/Gas 7. Have ready a roasting tray that's relatively non-stick (if in doubt, line it with baking paper).

Put the asparagus and lettuce halves into the roasting tray, trickle over the extra virgin olive oil and toss to coat. Cook in the oven for 4 minutes.

Take out the tray, move the veg to create gaps for the eggs and crack them into the spaces. Season with salt and pepper then return to the oven for 4–6 minutes until the egg whites are just cooked but the yolks are still runny. Serve at once.

Swaps
Try tenderstem or purple sprouting broccoli instead of the asparagus.

Crispy potatoes with bacon, tomatoes and spinach

This substantial breakfast, cooked all in one tray, is a great start to the day on a lazy weekend. Choosing good-quality bacon makes all the difference. I use unsmoked dry-cured streaky bacon which releases just a little tasty fat as it cooks and none of that white residue you get with cheap bacon. Getting golden crispy edges on the potatoes is also key to this dish.

Serves 2

500g new potatoes (skin on), halved
4 rashers of unsmoked streaky bacon, cut into 2cm pieces
1 tbsp sunflower oil
200g cherry tomatoes
100g spinach (tougher stalks removed and roughly chopped if using large leaf spinach)
Sea salt and freshly cracked black pepper

Preheat the oven to 220°C/210°C Fan/Gas 7.

Put the new potatoes and bacon into a roasting tray, add the sunflower oil and toss to mix. Season with salt and pepper, going easy on the salt as the bacon will contribute plenty. Cook in the oven for 10 minutes.

Take the tray from the oven and stir the potatoes around to coat in the fat released by the bacon. Return to the oven for 5 minutes, then remove and toss again. Repeat this until the potatoes are golden and crispy (around another 15 minutes).

Add the cherry tomatoes to the roasting tray and return to the oven for 5 minutes or until their skins are just starting to break.

Now add the spinach and toss through the potatoes. Pop the tray back in the oven for 2 minutes or until the spinach is wilted. Taste to check the seasoning – it may need an extra crack of pepper and a pinch more salt – then you're ready to go.

Swaps
Try Baby Gem lettuce leaves instead of spinach – they will retain a little extra crunch. Any leftover cooked potatoes can be used for this dish.

Spicy beans, greens and yoghurt

This protein-packed breakfast will set you up perfectly for a busy day. The beans were roasted in a clay oven in Mexico the first time I tasted this dish. I fell in love with it, and have replicated it as best I can. Feel free to up the spice level to suit your taste. Any leftovers can be fried and served in tortilla wraps for lunch the following day.

Serves 4

1 medium onion, finely chopped
3 garlic cloves, finely chopped
2 tbsp sunflower oil
1 tbsp paprika
½ tsp smoked paprika
1 medium-hot chilli, deseeded
   and finely chopped
1 tbsp tamari (or soy sauce)
400g tin chopped tomatoes
30g tomato purée
400g tin kidney beans, drained
   and rinsed
400g tin black beans, drained
   and rinsed
400g tin haricot beans, drained
   and rinsed
150g kale, tough stalks removed,
   roughly chopped
Sea salt and freshly cracked
   black pepper

To serve
3–4 tbsp natural yoghurt
Buttered toast (optional)

Preheat the oven to 200°C/180°C Fan/Gas 6.

Put the onion and garlic into a roasting tray, trickle with the sunflower oil and toss to coat. Cook in the oven for 5 minutes until the onion starts to take on a little colour.

Take out the tray and turn the oven down to 150°C/130°C Fan/Gas 2. Add the rest of the ingredients, except the kale, seasoning with some salt and pepper. Stir to combine and return to the oven. Cook for 40 minutes, stirring halfway through.

Add the kale to the mix and stir through. If the beans are a bit dry, add a splash of water too. Return to the oven for 10 minutes or until the kale is tender and cooked down. Taste to check the seasoning.

Serve piping hot with a good dollop of yoghurt. Buttered toast is optional... but only just!

Swaps
Butter beans work well in place of the haricot beans. And any greens can be introduced instead of the kale – spinach is particularly good and needs little time to cook, just a few minutes until it is wilted.

Roast pearl barley and smoked fish kedgeree

Kedgeree has long been a River Cottage favourite and, as with everything we do at the farm, we've tinkered with it many times. These days we prefer to use barley or spelt grown in the UK rather than imported rice. This version is often cooked as a staff meal to fuel our chefs through the day – that it all happens in the oven suits a busy, bustling kitchen.

Serves 4

1 medium onion, finely chopped
2 garlic cloves, finely chopped
½ fennel bulb, finely sliced
1 tbsp sunflower oil
300g pearl barley, pre-soaked (for at least 30 minutes, preferably 2 hours)
1 tbsp good-quality medium-hot curry powder
1 tsp ground coriander
1 tsp ground cumin
1 litre veg stock
100ml double cream
100g spinach (tougher stalks removed and roughly chopped if using large leaf spinach)
A small bunch of coriander, roughly chopped
200g MSC-certified smoked white fish fillet, such as haddock, skinned
4 medium eggs
Sea salt and freshly cracked black pepper

Preheat the oven to 200°C/180°C Fan/Gas 6.

Put the onion, garlic and fennel into a roasting tray, add the sunflower oil and toss to coat. Place in the oven for 5 minutes until the veg start to take on a little colour.

Drain the pearl barley and add to the roasting tray with the curry powder, ground coriander, cumin and half the veg stock. Stir well and return to the oven for 10 minutes.

Take out the tray and check the pearl barley: it should have just started to tenderise; add a little more stock if it is a little dry. Return to the oven for a further 10 minutes. Check the barley again, add the rest of the veg stock and stir. Bake for a further 10 minutes or until the barley is fully tender and all the stock is absorbed.

Add the cream, spinach and coriander to the roasting tray, stir through and season with salt and pepper. Return to the oven for 2–3 minutes until the spinach is wilted. In the meantime, cut the smoked fish into 2cm pieces.

Add the smoked fish to the kedgeree and stir gently, then make 4 hollows in the mix with the back of a spoon. Crack the eggs into these and season them with salt and pepper. Return the roasting tray to the oven for 4–6 minutes until the fish is just cooked and the egg whites are just set but the yolks are still runny. Serve straight away.

Swaps
Try using smoked mackerel fillet instead of white fish for a more intense flavour.

Baked beans, sausages and tomatoes

I couldn't have a breakfast chapter without the great British banger, but as with everything, quality is all-important here. Choose great butcher's sausages, steering well clear of mass-produced varieties. This hearty breakfast also includes a speedy way to make your own 'baked beans'. I'm hoping it will be enough to convince you to ditch the familiar tinned sugar-laden alternative.

Serves 4

8 large pork sausages
6 ripe medium tomatoes, halved
2 tbsp olive oil
4 small vines of cherry tomatoes, or 500g loose cherry tomatoes
2 garlic cloves, roughly chopped
1 tsp smoked paprika
½ tsp cayenne pepper
2 x 400g tins butter beans, well drained
400g tin chopped tomatoes
1 tbsp tomato purée
Sea salt and freshly cracked black pepper
Freshly toasted bread, to serve

Preheat the oven to 220°C/210°C Fan/Gas 7.

Place the sausages and halved tomatoes in a roasting tray and trickle over the olive oil. Season with salt and pepper and cook in the oven for 10 minutes, turning the sausages after 5 minutes.

Add the cherry tomatoes and garlic and cook for a further 6–7 minutes, until the tomato skins just start to break. Take the tray from the oven and lift out the sausages and cherry tomatoes, setting them aside on a plate.

Add the smoked paprika, cayenne, butter beans, tinned tomatoes and tomato purée to the tray and stir to mix with the roasted tomatoes until they break down and form a sauce. Return the tray to the oven for 5 minutes until the mixture starts to bubble.

Taste to check the seasoning of the sauce, adding a little more salt and pepper if necessary. Return the sausages and cherry tomatoes to the mix and cook in the oven for another 2–3 minutes.

Serve piping hot, with plenty of toast to hand.

Swaps
Replace the pork sausages with chunky lardons of smoked streaky bacon, or nice big field mushrooms for a veggie alternative.

Chorizo, eggs and onions with green herbs

Our homemade 'chorizo' is an inexpensive and incredibly versatile way to get that rich chorizo flavour into a dish. It keeps well for up to 7 days, so I'd recommend making double the quantity and keeping the rest in a sealed container in the fridge. You can pop it into pasta sauces, scatter it on top of pizzas or add it to pretty much anything savoury to lift it.

Serves 4

For our homemade 'chorizo'
250g coarsely minced fatty pork
1 tsp smoked paprika
1 tsp sweet paprika
1 tsp fennel seeds, toasted
2 garlic cloves, finely chopped
A splash of red wine
A pinch of cayenne pepper, or to taste
3g salt

For the finished dish
3 medium onions, quartered
A bunch of spring onions, trimmed and cut into 2cm pieces
8 medium eggs
A small bunch of flat-leaf parsley, leaves picked and chopped
A small bunch of dill, roughly chopped
A few sprigs of coriander, leaves picked and chopped
A few sprigs of tarragon, leaves picked and chopped
Sea salt and freshly cracked black pepper

To finish and serve
Sprigs of dill and coriander
Mayonnaise

To prepare the 'chorizo', mix all the ingredients together in a bowl, cover and allow to stand in a cool place for at least a couple of hours, preferably overnight.

Preheat the oven to 220°C/210°C Fan/Gas 7.

Put the onions and spring onions into a roasting tray, about 25 x 15cm. Break the chorizo into large lumps and scatter over the onions. Cook in the oven for 10 minutes, then take out and stir vigorously, breaking up the lumps of chorizo. Return to the oven for 10 minutes.

Meanwhile, crack the eggs into a large bowl, add the chopped herbs and season with a good twist of pepper and a little salt, bearing in mind that the chorizo will lend salt to the overall dish.

Remove the tray from the oven, pour the herby egg over the chorizo and onion mixture and stir together. Place back in the oven and cook for 10 minutes. Pierce the centre of the mixture with a knife to check for any runny egg: if there is any, pop it back in the oven until it is cooked all the way through.

Finish with a scattering of dill and coriander. Serve hot, with a good dollop of mayonnaise. This is also good cold, so save any leftovers for your lunchbox.

Swaps
Try adding a handful of grated cheese to the herby egg mix. You can also use cherry tomatoes or chopped larger tomatoes in place of the chorizo for a veggie option.

Black pudding with yoghurt, lettuce, grapes and toast

Black pudding is divisive: you either love it or hate it. I think those who dislike it have only ever tasted the poor-quality version, which is widely available (but not really worth eating). A good black pudding – packed with lovely ingredients – is a joy to eat. The one we make at the farm is enriched with cream, brandy and paprika. Here it forms the basis of an unusual but delicious breakfast.

Serves 4

2 Baby Gem lettuce, quartered
    lengthways
200g good-quality black pudding,
    cut into 2cm pieces
2 tbsp cold-pressed rapeseed oil
4 generous slices of sourdough
2 tbsp extra virgin olive oil
100g green grapes, halved and
    pips removed
100g natural yoghurt
Sea salt and freshly cracked
    black pepper

Preheat the oven to 220°C/210°C Fan/Gas 7.

Place the lettuce cut side up on a roasting tray, scatter over the black pudding and trickle the rapeseed oil over everything. Season with salt and pepper and cook in the oven for 10 minutes.

Meanwhile, lay the sourdough slices on a baking tray, trickle over half the extra virgin olive oil and season with salt and pepper. Now turn the bread over and repeat on the other side.

Pop the tray in the oven with the black pudding. Check after 4–5 minutes to see if the underside of the bread is golden brown: if so turn the slices over; if not return to the oven for a little longer before flipping them over. Cook until both sides are golden.

Once the black pudding tray has had 10 minutes in the oven, toss in the grapes and cook for a further 5 minutes.

Remove the toast when it is ready and place on serving plates. Add the black pudding, grapes and lettuce. Dollop the yoghurt on top and grind over some pepper to serve.

Swaps
Gooseberries work nicely instead of grapes while in season, and if you don't fancy black pudding you can use whole roast chestnuts or chunks of smoked tofu instead.

Toasty seedy granola

A bowl of granola is an ever-popular turn-to breakfast but packet versions are often loaded with sugar. This version gives you control over what goes in and you can vary the ingredients as you like. I particularly like the hit of spicy warmth the stem ginger gives, along with the crunch of the pumpkin seeds and the sweetness of the dried apple.

10–12 servings

300g porridge oats
50g rye flakes
50g wheat flakes
50g pumpkin seeds
50g light muscovado sugar
100g butter, softened, in pieces
50g treacle
1 medium egg, beaten
2 pieces of preserved stem ginger, drained and finely chopped
100g dried apple, finely chopped

To finish and serve
Natural yoghurt or kefir
Raspberries or other soft fruit (optional)

Preheat the oven to 190°C/170°C Fan/Gas 5.

Tip the oats, rye and wheat flakes into a baking tray, spread out evenly and cook in the oven for 10 minutes.

Take out the tray, add the rest of the ingredients and mix well. Return to the oven for 8 minutes, stirring halfway through. Remove and set aside to cool.

This granola will keep in an airtight jar for a couple of weeks. Serve it with a generous dollop of yoghurt or kefir, and summer berries when they're in season.

Swaps
You can use any cereal flakes in place of the wheat and rye. And any mixture of dried fruit can be used in place of the apple and ginger – apricots work particularly well.

Spiced apple compote with apricots and toasted cereals

Roasting the apples for this compote means you don't need to add any water, so that good old Bramley flavour is wonderfully intense. As I'm a sucker for Bramley's brilliant sharpness – and the apricots lend enough sweetness for me – I don't add sugar, but if you like a sweeter note, substitute half of the Bramleys with eating apples.

Serves 4

1kg Bramley apples
150g unsulphured dried apricots, roughly chopped
200g mixed cereal flakes, such as rye, wheat and oat
20g pumpkin seeds
20g sunflower seeds
Natural yoghurt, to serve (optional)

Preheat the oven to 220°C/200°C Fan/Gas 7

Peel, quarter and core the apples and place them in a roasting dish with the dried apricots. Stir to mix and cook in the oven for 15–20 minutes.

Take out the roasting dish and stir the mixture to break up the apples and form a rough, saucy compote. Sprinkle over the cereal flakes and seeds and return to the oven for 5 minutes. Serve hot, with a dollop of natural yoghurt, if you like.

Swaps
Substitute half the Bramleys with pears or grated quince.

All-in-the-oven eggy bread with summer berries

I love eggy bread, not least because it brings back fond childhood memories. These days I do it all in the oven, because I can fit enough for us all in one baking tray, which means we all get to eat it hot and together and I don't have to stand over a hot stove. A win-win!

Serves 4

4 medium eggs
100ml whole milk
½ tsp ground cinnamon
A couple of gratings of nutmeg
8 thick slices of slightly stale
   wholemeal bread
A large knob of butter
About 150g berries in season,
   such as strawberries, blueberries
   and raspberries

Preheat the oven to 210°C/190°C Fan/Gas 6½. Place a baking tray in the oven to heat up.

Beat the eggs, milk, cinnamon and nutmeg together in a bowl, then pour into a (cold) tray or large shallow dish. Place the slices of bread in the beaten egg mix for a couple of minutes, then turn the bread slices over and allow them to soak up the rest of the egg mixture.

Take the hot tray from the oven, add the butter and let it melt. Lay the soaked bread slices in the tray and cook in the oven for 4 minutes. Take out the tray and flip the bread slices over, then return to the oven for a further 4 minutes.

Scatter the berries over the eggy bread. I like to pop the tray back in the oven for a few minutes before serving – until the berries just start to soften.

Swaps
For a more American-style breakfast, swap the berries for slices of crispy streaky bacon and a trickle of honey.

Roast plums with star anise, oats and kefir

Plums are one of our finest homegrown fruits, but their season is short, so we need to make the most of it. There are lots of varieties worth exploring with unique and interesting flavours, and if you embrace them you can enjoy plums from mid-summer through to early autumn. Here I'm using Victoria plums – a good 'all-rounder' that's easy to get hold of from late August onward.

Serves 4

1kg Victoria plums, halved
   and stoned
4 star anise
1 tbsp light muscovado sugar
50g porridge oats
Kefir or natural yoghurt, to serve

Preheat the oven to 200°C/180°C Fan/Gas 6.

Place the plums in a roasting dish with the star anise and sugar and stir together. Roast in the oven for between 5 and 10 minutes, depending on the ripeness of the plums. As soon as they start to soften and puff up a little, remove from the oven.

Scatter over the oats, return to the oven and cook for a further 5 minutes, or until the plums are soft and starting to break down and the oats are taking on a little colour.

Serve with a good splash of kefir or a dollop of yoghurt, not forgetting to remove the star anise.

Swaps
Peaches are a delicious swap for the plums.

2
SNACKY THINGS

Snacking should never be a guilty pleasure. It should just be a pleasure. But the problem is it can be hard to buy really good snacks, since they're so often loaded with salt and extra fat (as well as wrapped in bits of plastic). But when you make them yourself, you have total control of what goes into them, in a way you just can't when you buy manufactured foods.

The snacks here range from the kind of thing you want when you sit down to watch a film – or pack for a picnic – to nibbles to serve with drinks. We've taken old favourites and shaken them up: think potato wedges, but with sumac and harissa (on page 45); 'twiglets', but with miso and soy sauce (on page 58); mini baked potatoes, stuffed with goat's cheese and herbs (on page 50); salt and vinegar, but on crunchy peas and beans (see page 57) rather than crisps.

If you love grilled cheese sandwiches but hate sandwich toasters that drip grease on to the counter and are a devil to clean, you'll enjoy our new and improved Oven-roasted cheese toasties (page 53). And because our chicken and chips are baked, not fried, they're made with less fat, too (see pages 49 and 54).

Many of the snacks here can be batched and stored – although even when we make double or triple quantities, we often find they disappear before we get the chance to stash them away. These are snacks, made better... give them a go.

Raid-the-fridge frittata

This is a great way to use up leftovers, as long as you have some eggs and cheese to hand. Here I've used new potatoes, red onion, mushrooms, tomatoes and kale, but you can have pretty much any combination and throw in some herbs if you like. It's always good to have something green in there, and if you include meat make sure it's cut into smallish pieces. This is such a useful recipe, I make it more or less on a weekly basis.

Serves 4

500g leftover cooked veg and/
    or meat or fish
8 cherry tomatoes (optional)
8 medium eggs, beaten
200g Cheddar (or other cheese),
    grated
Sea salt and freshly cracked
    black pepper

Preheat the oven to 220°C/200°C Fan/Gas 7. Line the base of a shallow roasting tray, about 25 x 15cm, with baking paper.

Chop or slice the leftovers. Tip them into the roasting tray, with the cherry tomatoes if using, and spread out evenly. Pour on the beaten eggs, season liberally with salt and pepper and scatter over the grated cheese. Stir lightly to combine.

Cook in the oven for 15 minutes or until the egg is set. Pierce the centre of the frittata with the tip of a knife to check there is no runny egg – if there is, return the tray to the oven, checking every 5 minutes.

Remove the frittata from the oven and cut into squares to serve. It's delicious served hot but also good eaten cold – ideal for lunchboxes or picnics.

Swaps
You can use any cheese you have in the fridge, or a mix. It's particularly good with a little crumbled blue cheese thrown in.

Sumac potato wedges with soured cream and harissa dip

These are perfect for a movie night, and so much nicer than chips.
Sumac lends a beautiful citrussy flavour with a little chilli heat. Make
sure you use the right kind of potato, not just a generic 'all-rounder' –
it will make all the difference and you'll get those lovely crispy edges,
which are the best bits.

Serves 4

4 large floury potatoes, such as
 King Edward or Maris Piper
 (skin on)
3 tbsp sunflower or rapeseed oil
1 tbsp sumac
Flaky sea salt and freshly cracked
 black pepper

For the dip
200g soured cream (or natural
 yoghurt)
1 tbsp good-quality rose harissa

To serve
A large handful of coriander

Preheat the oven to 230°C/220°C Fan/Gas 8.

Cut the potatoes lengthways into 2.5cm thick wedges.
Bring a large pan of water to the boil, add the potato
wedges and boil for 7–10 minutes. Drain well and leave
to steam-dry in the colander for 5 minutes.

Put the oil into a shallow roasting tray and place in the
oven for 4–5 minutes, until smoking hot.

Add the potato wedges to the roasting tray, turn to coat
in the hot oil and season with flaky sea salt. Roast in the
oven for 10 minutes. Take out the tray and turn the potato
wedges then return to the oven for a further 5 minutes.

For the dip, put the soured cream (or yoghurt) into
a serving dish and stir through the rose harissa.

Remove the tray from the oven and sprinkle the potato
wedges with the sumac and some black pepper, plus
a little salt if you think they need it. Scatter over the
coriander and serve with the soured cream dip.

Swaps
Try using parsnips instead of potatoes, par-boiling them
for just 2–3 minutes as they take less time to cook.

Spiced roasted carrot and orange hummus

We make a lot of hummus at River Cottage, but rarely with chickpeas.
This root-veg-based version is a firm favourite, and the addition of orange
really lifts the spices. It's great with crunchy veg, sourdough crackers or
warm garlicky flatbreads.

Serves 8 (as a nibble)

1kg carrots
1 orange
2 tsp cumin seeds
2 tsp coriander seeds
6 tbsp extra virgin olive oil or
   cold-pressed rapeseed oil,
   plus extra to finish
2 garlic cloves, finely chopped
Juice of 1 lemon
3 tbsp tahini (or peanut butter)
Sea salt and freshly cracked
   black pepper
100g toasted seeds, such as
   sunflower or pumpkin, to finish

Preheat the oven to 220°C/200°C Fan/Gas 7.

Cut the carrots into 2.5cm chunks and place in a shallow
roasting tray. Finely grate the zest from the orange over
the carrots.

Place the zested orange on a board and slice off the top
and bottom, then cut away all the white pith. Cut the
orange flesh into chunks, discarding any pips as you go,
and add to the roasting tray.

Add the spice seeds, oil and garlic and toss to mix with
the carrots and orange. Cook in the oven for 15 minutes,
then take out the tray and give everything a good stir.
Return to the oven and cook for a further 10 minutes or
until the carrots are completely tender.

Remove the tray from the oven and scrape the contents
into a freestanding blender. Add the lemon juice and
tahini (or peanut butter). Pulse, adding a splash of water
if needed to blitz, and keeping some texture rather than
blending the mixture until smooth. Season with salt and
pepper to taste.

Scrape the hummus into a serving bowl and top with a
sprinkling of toasted seeds and a trickle of your chosen oil.

Swaps
Try using beetroot instead of carrots. Prepare as above,
throwing a good handful of pumpkin seeds into the
roasting tray with the beetroot and orange. (Beetroot
are a little more watery than carrots and the seeds will
thicken the hummus nicely.)

Tony's slow-roasted curried chicken legs

This is my father-in-law Tony's recipe. He had ten kids to feed and my incredible partner was one of them. This reminds her of long family walks when Tony would pack these chicken pieces to eat on the way. It's such a simple recipe but delicious, and the response I get from everyone when I cook it always fills me with joy... especially from the one it means so much to. Hopefully it will make you as happy as it does my crazy family!

Serves 4

4 chicken drumsticks
4 chicken thighs
1 generous tbsp good-quality
   curry powder
3 tbsp sunflower oil
Sea salt and freshly cracked
   black pepper

Preheat the oven to 180°C/160°C Fan/Gas 4.

Place the chicken pieces in a large bowl with the curry powder, some salt and pepper and the sunflower oil. Toss to coat the chicken well then transfer to a roasting dish or tray, placing the pieces skin side up (or the side with most skin uppermost).

Cook in the oven for 1½ hours until the skin is crisp and the meat is very tender. Don't be tempted to rush the cooking – if you do, you won't get that crispy skin. Serve hot or cold.

Swaps
For a more indulgent take, replace the chicken pieces with 7cm cubes of belly pork, or roast a combination of chicken and pork.

New potatoes stuffed with chives and goat's cheese

These are a real favourite in our house and I often make them when we have guests around, or for those cosy movie nights. They're also great to take out and about on picnics or walks, or to pack into lunchboxes. I think of them as brilliant little snacks to be brought out on any occasion.

Makes 30 (bite-size)

15 medium new potatoes
(skin on)
2 tbsp extra virgin olive oil
150g soft goat's cheese
A small bunch of chives
(about 20g), finely snipped
Sea salt and freshly cracked
black pepper

Preheat the oven to 220°C/210°C Fan/Gas 7.

Place the potatoes in a shallow roasting tray, trickle over the extra virgin olive oil and turn to coat. Season well with salt and pepper. Roast in the oven for 25–35 minutes depending on size, until tender. To test, protecting your hand (as they'll be hot), gently squeeze the sides of a potato and you should feel it just break apart under the skin. Leave until cool enough to handle comfortably.

Cut each potato in half and gently scoop out the flesh into a bowl, being careful to leave the skin intact. Place the empty potato skins back on the roasting tray, cavity side up.

Add the goat's cheese and chives to the potato flesh, mix well and season with salt and pepper to taste. Spoon the mixture into the potato skins, dividing it evenly. Return to the oven for 5–10 minutes (allow 10 minutes for crispy browned tops).

Leave the potatoes to stand for a few minutes to cool a little before serving. Any leftovers will keep for a couple of days in the fridge and can be reheated or eaten cold.

Swaps
Use Maris Pipers or King Edwards to make super-sized stuffed potatoes. Obviously, they'll take a lot longer to cook: 45 minutes – 1 hour to soften enough to scoop out, but they make an excellent supper, served with a salad.

Oven-roasted cheese toasties

I love a cheese toastie, especially one that dispenses with the need for a toasted sandwich maker and the grease that seeps out of it! You can't use good bread in one of those machines either, because it's impossible to shut the lid on it. With this all-in-the-oven version you can use great bread and cook enough toasted sarnies for everyone in one go – so you can all sit and eat together.

Serves 4

8 slices of good-quality
   wholemeal bread
Butter, to spread
150g mature Cheddar, sliced
150g mild Cheddar, sliced
2 tomatoes, thinly sliced
4 tbsp piccalilli

Preheat the oven to 250°C/240°C Fan/Gas 10, or as hot as it will go.

Spread the slices of bread with butter. Lay half of them, buttered side down, in a shallow roasting tray and cook in the oven for 3–5 minutes.

Take the tray from the oven and lay the slices of mature and mild Cheddar on the bread slices. Place the tomato slices on top and spread the piccalilli evenly over the tomatoes. Cover with the remaining bread slices, placing them buttered side uppermost. Press down firmly (you will get slightly buttery hands).

Return the tray to the oven for a further 6–8 minutes until the cheese is fully melted within the toasties. Tuck in straight away.

Swaps
For a stronger flavour, try using a tangy blue cheese, such as Blue Vinny, instead of the mature Cheddar. Any chutney will work in place of the piccalilli – you just need some acidity to cut through the richness of the cheese.

Ripped oven chips with smoked chilli and roasted garlic dip

We are a nation of chip lovers, but it's a bit of a faff (and smelly) to deep-fry chips at home. This roasted new potato version is much easier and the smoky, garlicky, spicy mayo is the perfect accompanying dip. You can make it a day or two ahead and keep it in the fridge until ready to serve.

Serves 6

For the chips
15 good-sized new potatoes
   (skin on)
3 tbsp sunflower oil
3 sprigs of rosemary, torn
   into pieces
Flaky sea salt and freshly cracked
   black pepper

For the dip
2 egg yolks
2 tsp Dijon mustard
1 tsp dried chipotle chilli flakes
1 roasted garlic bulb (see page 180),
   soft flesh squeezed from skin
2 tsp cider vinegar
Juice of ½ lemon
125ml extra virgin olive oil
125ml light rapeseed or
   sunflower oil

Put the potatoes into a large pan of lightly salted water and bring to the boil. Lower the heat and cook until the potatoes are just softened in the middle; this will take 20–30 minutes depending on the size and potato variety. Drain well and leave to steam-dry in the colander until cool enough to handle comfortably.

Meanwhile, make the dip. Put the egg yolks, mustard, chilli flakes, roasted garlic, cider vinegar and lemon juice into a small food processor and blitz briefly to combine. Then, with the motor running, slowly add the oils, a few drips at a time to start with, then in a thin trickle. The mayo will thicken as more oil is added. (Alternatively, you can make the mayo by hand in a large bowl, using a stiff whisk.) Season with salt and pepper to taste.

Preheat the oven to 240°C/230°C Fan/Gas 9. Rip the potatoes from the small ends downwards to create uneven wedges with rough sides (this is where all the brilliant crispy edges will form on roasting).

Put the sunflower oil into a shallow roasting tray and place in the hot oven for 5 minutes to heat up. Carefully tip the ripped potatoes into the hot tray, season with salt and pepper and turn to coat in the oil. Spread the potatoes out in a single layer and roast in the oven for 5 minutes.

Take out the tray, turn the potatoes and add the rosemary. Return to the oven for a further 5–10 minutes until the ripped chips are nice and crispy. Using a slotted spoon, transfer the potatoes to a tray lined with kitchen paper to drain off any excess oil. Season with flaky salt and serve at once, with the dip.

Seaweed, salt and vinegar peas and beans

An ideal nibble for any occasion – and much more interesting than shop-bought crisps or Bombay mix. All you need is a couple of good handfuls of dried beans and peas, a few flavourings and patience. These are my favourite flavouring ingredients, but you can play around with others once you have the technique sorted.

6–8 servings

200g dried split fava beans,
   soaked for at least 2 hours
200g dried marrowfat peas,
   soaked for at least 2 hours
6 tbsp sunflower oil
6 tbsp dried seaweed flakes
   (preferably dulse)
8 tbsp cider vinegar
Sea salt and freshly cracked
   black pepper

Bring a couple of medium saucepans of water to the boil. Drain the beans and add the fava beans to one pan and the marrowfat peas to the other. Bring to the boil and cook until tender but not breaking apart: allow around 45 minutes for fava beans; about 25 minutes for the marrowfat peas. Drain well and allow to cool.

Preheat the oven to 170°C/150°C Fan/Gas 3.

Tip the beans and peas into a shallow roasting tray, trickle over the sunflower oil and season with salt and pepper. Toss gently to mix. Spread the peas and beans out in the tray, making sure they are in a single layer. Roast in the oven for 25 minutes until they are starting to crisp up.

Take out the tray and stir through the seaweed flakes and cider vinegar. Return to the oven for 12–15 minutes or until the beans and peas are golden and crispy all over, checking and gently stirring at around 8 minutes and again a few minutes later.

Remove from the oven and allow to cool slightly then taste to check the seasoning. You can serve this snack warm from the oven or leave it to cool and store in an airtight container for up to 2 weeks.

Swaps
Try adding 1 tsp curry powder with the oil and seasoning to get somewhere close to Bombay mix.

Roast sourdough and seed twigs

This take on ever-popular Twiglets is a fun way to use up excess sourdough starter. But don't worry if you haven't got one on the go, I've given an alternative. Rather than relying solely on yeast extract to flavour these, I add miso and soy sauce to create a deeper flavour. This recipe makes a lot but that's because I find they get eaten as quickly as I can bake them!

Makes about 100

150g sourdough starter
  (or 75g white bread flour
  mixed with 75ml water and
  ½ tsp fast-action dried yeast
  and left to stand for 1 hour)
200g fine wholemeal flour, plus
  extra to dust
1 tsp baking powder
A pinch of salt
50ml tepid water
40g tamari (or soy sauce)
2 tsp miso
20g sesame seeds
10g fast-action dried yeast
2 tsp yeast extract, plus extra
  to glaze
1 tbsp sunflower or light
  rapeseed oil

Mix all the ingredients together thoroughly in a large bowl until evenly blended and knead lightly to bring the dough together. Cover with a damp cloth and leave to rise in a warm spot for at least 1 hour.

Preheat the oven to 180°C/160°C Fan/Gas 4. Line 2 large baking trays with baking paper.

Tear off small pieces of dough, shape into little balls and roll out on a lightly floured surface with the palm of your hand to form thin sticks, about 5mm thick. These may break naturally as you roll, which is fine; if not, break them into 7–10cm lengths.

Place the slim dough sticks on the lined roasting trays, leaving about 1cm between each. Cook in the oven, one tray at a time, for 10 minutes until crispy.

Meanwhile, mix a little yeast extract with a tiny splash of water. Brush this glaze over the sticks and return to the oven for 5–10 minutes until the glaze is set. Leave to cool completely before serving. These savoury sticks will keep in an airtight tin for up to a week.

Swaps
For a spicier version, use Worcestershire sauce instead of soy sauce.

Crunchy spiced chickpeas

This is a super-easy way to create a protein-rich, scrumptious bowl of joy without much time or effort. Perfect for a little snack at any time of the day! I love the addition of cumin and caraway (which are related but taste quite different), as they add warmth but not overpowering flavour.

6–8 servings

2 x 400g tins chickpeas,
   drained and rinsed
1 tbsp ground cumin
1 tbsp ground caraway
A pinch of cayenne pepper
6 sprigs of thyme, leaves picked
2 tbsp sunflower or light
   rapeseed oil
Sea salt and freshly cracked
   black pepper

Preheat the oven to 200°C/180°C Fan/Gas 6.

Put all of the ingredients in a bowl, seasoning with some salt and pepper. Mix well to coat the chickpeas with the flavourings and oil. Tip into a baking tray and spread out into a single layer.

Cook in the oven for about 35 minutes until lovely and crunchy, stirring halfway through. Taste to check the seasoning, adding a little more salt and pepper if needed. Let cool slightly.

Serve the chickpeas warm from the oven or allow to cool completely before eating. They will keep for up to 2 weeks in an airtight container.

Swaps
Pretty much any ground spice will work with these roasted chickpeas.

Fennel pork crackling

Crunchy, crispy crackling is a real treat. We raise pigs on the farm at River Cottage and when they are butchered we utilise every last scrap of them, including the pig skin. This is a great use for it. In a sealed jar, the crackling will keep for a couple of days but you'll probably find it is eaten by the time it's fully cooled. A good butcher should be able to supply you with organic pig skin, or you can get it online.

Serves 6–8

500g organic pig skin
1 tbsp fennel seeds
A few sprigs of fennel flowers
   (if available)
Sea salt

Preheat the oven to 210°C/190°C Fan/Gas 6½.

Trim any excess fat from the underside of the pig skin (this can be rendered down and kept for roasting veg). Cut the skin into 1cm strips and place in a bowl. Lightly crush the fennel seeds, using a pestle and mortar. Add to the pig skin with a generous pinch of salt and mix well together.

Lay the pork skin strips, skin side up, on a wire rack over a roasting tray to catch any excess fat. Cook in the oven for 10 minutes, then turn the strips over, and add the fresh fennel flowers if using. Return to the oven for a further 5–10 minutes until the skin is fully crackled and crunchy.

Leave until cool enough to handle before serving.

Swaps
Try using coriander seeds or sumac in place of the fennel seeds; both work well.

Chilli, honey and soy roasted nuts and seeds

Salty, sweet and spicy, what more do you want from a snack! Using a mix of nuts and seeds gives you a lovely variety of flavours and textures. I leave these a bit sticky, but you can roast them a bit longer for a drier version if you like. The mix also makes an excellent addition to a salad, and is delicious sprinkled over roast veg.

Serves 6–8

50g hazelnuts
50g walnuts
30g sesame seeds
100g pumpkin seeds
100g sunflower seeds
100ml tamari (or soy sauce)
50g honey
½ tsp dried chipotle chilli flakes or more, to taste
Sea salt and freshly cracked black pepper

Preheat the oven to 180°C/160°C Fan/Gas 4.

Mix all the ingredients together in a bowl, seasoning with salt and pepper to taste. Tip into a shallow roasting tray and spread out to ensure they are in a single layer. Toast in the oven for 5 minutes.

Take out the tray, give everything a good stir and return to the oven for a further 5 minutes, or until the mix is sticky and starting to clump together.

Remove from the oven and give it one more stir then set aside to cool before serving. The nuts and seeds should remain a little sticky – this is when they are at their best.

Swaps
Vary the mixture of nuts and seeds for a different result every time – try including pecans and almonds, for example. A sprinkling of crushed cumin seeds is another lovely addition.

3
ONE-TRAY WONDERS

These are proper main meals – all conveniently cooked in one tray or dish in the oven and needing little else. Pop everything in the oven, leave it to cook and within an hour (much less if you're cooking fish), dinner is ready. With these recipes, there's no need to make sides – it really is the easiest kind of cooking. Easy doesn't mean basic though. I reckon you'd be happy to serve my Roast fish with broccoli, chilli, lemon and pumpkin seeds (page 70) or Creamy summer veg roast (page 86) at any dinner party.

Pulses feature strongly too. I use these a lot in my cooking, so I've always got a stack of jars and tins, ready to go. Of course, you can cook pulses from scratch but when I want some, chances are I won't have time to soak them overnight. I want to be able to cook things like Courgettes and chickpeas with tomatoes, harissa and mozzarella (page 82) straight away, so I use tinned pulses often.

We cook and eat a lot of plant-based food at River Cottage, so this chapter has plenty of meat-free dishes, including Sweetcorn with tomato, halloumi and smoked chilli (page 78), a spin on a dish we often cook for guests here, and Roast lettuce, spinach and peas with herby breadcrumbs (page 81), which works so well. For a comforting stew on a chilly day, try my Roast mushrooms with beer and dumplings (page 91). It's full of satisfying deep flavours and wonderfully sustaining.

Smoked haddock with potatoes, spinach, cream and thyme

I love smoked fish and I'm fortunate enough to be able to smoke my own, but I appreciate this is unusual. Most good fishmongers and supermarket fish counters sell naturally smoked fish, which is pale yellow in colour. Avoid anything that is bright yellow, as this will have been dyed and most likely dipped in a smoke-flavoured cure rather than smoked properly.

If you have any leftovers (which I doubt), thin down with a little stock the next day for a hearty chowder-like lunch.

Serves 4

500g new potatoes (skin on)
2 tbsp extra virgin olive oil
2 leeks, trimmed and cut
    into 1cm slices
5 sprigs of thyme
200g spinach (tougher stalks
    removed and roughly chopped
    if using large leaf spinach)
400g MSC-certified smoked
    haddock fillets (or any smoked
    sustainably caught white fish),
    pin-boned and skinned
400ml double cream
A small glass of dry white wine
50g mature Cheddar, grated
20g pumpkin seeds
A pinch of paprika
Sea salt and freshly cracked
    black pepper

Preheat the oven to 220°C/200°C Fan/Gas 7.

Put the new potatoes into an ovenproof pan or roasting tray. Trickle over the extra virgin olive oil, season lightly with salt and pepper and toss to coat. Cook in the oven for 25–30 minutes until the potatoes are just softened all the way through.

Take the pan out and use the back of a fork to just break each potato. Add the leeks and thyme, stir and cook in the oven for 10 minutes. Now add the spinach and return to the oven for a couple of minutes until it is just wilted.

In the meantime, cut the fish into 2cm cubes. Remove the pan from the oven and add the smoked haddock, cream and white wine. Stir together and return to the oven for 12–15 minutes, until the fish is cooked.

Take out the pan again and turn the oven setting up to 230°C/220°C Fan/Gas 8. Sprinkle over the grated cheese, then the pumpkin seeds and paprika. Return to the oven for a few minutes until the cheese is melted and starting to brown. Serve at once.

Swaps
This works well if you replace the smoked fish with small or halved larger chestnut mushrooms.

Roast fish with broccoli, chilli, lemon and pumpkin seeds

I'm lucky to live so close to the coast and know some excellent fishermen. My friends Nigel, Corinne and Sam at our local fishmongers always provide me with the best fish – it helps they have their own boat! I don't get hung up on particular fish, I prefer to cook whatever is freshly caught. This is a quick and easy dish and enables you to have a restaurant-level dinner on the table in next to no time.

Serves 4

2 small heads of broccoli
  (about 750g)
2 lemons
2 garlic cloves, finely chopped
1 red chilli (or more for extra heat),
  deseeded and finely chopped
A small bunch of coriander
150g pumpkin seeds
4 tbsp cold-pressed rapeseed oil
4 fillets of hake or other sustainably
  caught white fish (about
  200g each)
Sea salt and freshly cracked
  black pepper

Preheat the oven to 210°C/190°C Fan/Gas 6½.

Cut the florets from the broccoli and halve the larger ones through their stem. Place in a large bowl. Peel the large broccoli stalk, cut into 2cm cubes and add to the florets.

Finely grate the zest from the lemons and add it to the broccoli with the garlic and chilli. (Save the zested lemons for later.) Pick the leaves from the coriander and add them to the broccoli; finely chop the coriander stems and add these too.

Throw in the pumpkin seeds, trickle over 3 tbsp of the rapeseed oil and season with salt and pepper. Toss to mix the broccoli with the flavourings, and then transfer to a shallow roasting tray and spread out.

Season the hake fillets with salt and pepper and place on top of the broccoli. Trickle over the remaining 1 tbsp rapeseed oil and roast in the oven for 12–15 minutes until the fish is cooked through. To test, pierce the thickest part of a fish fillet with the tip of a knife and check the flesh is opaque through to the middle.

Cut the lemons in half and squeeze the juice over the fish and broccoli. Serve straight away.

Swaps
Substitute the broccoli with tenderstem, purple sprouting, kalettes or halved Brussels sprouts.

Roast mackerel with fennel, apple and bay

Mackerel is my favourite oily fish and, as freshness is paramount, we are fortunate to have lots of it landed nearby at Lyme Regis. It's an ideal fish for roasting as the oily flesh stays succulent in the oven. Fennel is an excellent partner, along with apples and lemons which add a little acidity to cut through the richness. Working the mackerel flesh from the bones can be a bit messy so have plenty of napkins to hand. Just get stuck in!

Serves 2

2 medium line-caught mackerel,
   cleaned
2 tbsp extra virgin olive oil
2–3 small fennel bulbs, trimmed
2 small eating apples
1 lemon, sliced
8 bay leaves
3 sprigs of thyme
Sea salt and freshly cracked
   black pepper

Preheat the oven to 200°C/180°C Fan/Gas 6. Have the mackerel ready, at room temperature.

Quarter the fennel bulbs and place in a roasting tray. Trickle over the extra virgin olive oil and season with salt and pepper. Roast in the oven for 15 minutes.

In the meantime, halve or quarter the apples, depending on their size.

Scatter the apples, lemon slices and bay leaves over and around the fennel. Pick the leaves off the thyme sprigs and scatter over the fennel and apples. Stir the fennel and apple mix and spread out evenly in the roasting tray. Season the mackerel with salt and pepper and lay on top of the fennel.

Roast in the oven for about 15 minutes until the fish is cooked through. To test, pierce the thickest part of the biggest fish with the tip of a knife and check the flesh has changed colour all the way through. If not, return to the oven, checking every couple of minutes to make sure you don't overcook the fish. Serve hot from the oven.

Swaps

For an equally delicious (but slightly more fiddly) affair, replace the mackerel with fresh whole sardines: you'll need about 4 sardines per portion. Cook the fennel and apple mixture in the oven for 5 minutes before adding the sardines and cooking for another 8–10 minutes.

Courgettes, lentils, tomatoes, bacon and goat's cheese

Goat's cheese sits so well with flavourful tomatoes and delicate courgettes in this light, summery one-pan dish. Try to source a good English goat's cheese, like the one we get from nearby Fivepenny Farm, which is creamy and salty in satisfying proportions. This is a dish I come back to time and again, as I'm sure you will. Asparagus with spinach and roasted garlic butter (page 180) is a lovely accompaniment when asparagus is in season.

Serves 4

150g piece of streaky bacon, cut into cubes
A splash of sunflower oil (if needed)
3 medium courgettes, trimmed and cut into 2.5cm slices
1 tsp fennel seeds
1 tbsp tomato purée
400g tin chopped tomatoes
400g tin green lentils, drained and rinsed
200g cherry tomatoes
A bunch of basil, leaves picked and roughly torn
A small bunch of flat-leaf parsley, leaves picked and roughly chopped
200g soft goat's cheese
1 tsp smoked paprika
100g sunflower seeds
Sea salt and freshly cracked black pepper

Preheat the oven to 230°C/220°C Fan/Gas 8.

Put the bacon into an ovenproof pan or roasting tray and pop in the oven for 5 minutes, to allow the bacon to start to release some fat. If it doesn't you may need to add a little sunflower oil to the pan. Add the courgettes, stir and cook in the oven for 5 minutes.

Add the fennel seeds, tomato purée, tinned tomatoes, lentils, cherry tomatoes and chopped herbs. Season with salt and pepper and stir well. Return to the oven and cook for 15 minutes.

Take out the pan and give everything a good stir. Taste to check the seasoning and adjust as necessary. Dot the goat's cheese over the surface, sprinkle with the smoked paprika and scatter over the sunflower seeds. Return to the oven for 15 minutes or until the cheese is golden.

Serve piping hot, straight from the pan.

Swaps
Replace the bacon with pitted Kalamata olives, which lend a lovely earthy, salty tang.

Sausages with lentils and squash

This is a great family supper, and with plenty of veggies it's a pretty healthy one too. It doesn't even need mash or anything else on the side, as the lentils make it really satisfying. You can use apple juice or veg stock instead of the cider to make it alcohol-free if you like.

Serves 4

8 large butcher's pork sausages
650g squash, such as Crown Prince or butternut, peeled and deseeded
12–15 small shallots, peeled (or 2 medium onions, diced)
3 tbsp sunflower oil
3 garlic cloves, finely sliced
3 medium carrots, finely chopped
2 celery sticks, finely chopped
3 sprigs of thyme
400g tin chopped tomatoes
400g tin green lentils, drained
500ml bottle of dry cider
3 tbsp tomato purée
A small bunch of flat-leaf parsley, leaves picked and roughly chopped
Sea salt and freshly cracked black pepper

Preheat the oven to 230°C/220°C Fan/Gas 8.

Place the sausages in a roasting tray. Cut the squash into 2.5cm cubes and add to the tray with the shallots (or onions). Trickle over the sunflower oil and toss to coat everything. Cook in the oven for about 20 minutes, stirring every 5 minutes, until the sausages are browned all over.

Take out the roasting tray and stir through the rest of the ingredients, seasoning with some salt and pepper. Return to the oven and cook for about 20 minutes, stirring halfway through, until the sauce is reduced to a lovely thick consistency and the sausages have started to peek out of the sauce and get a little crispy on top.

Remove from the oven, taste the sauce to check the seasoning and add more salt and pepper if needed. Serve piping hot – with a cold glass of the same cider you've cooked with!

Swaps
Replace the lentils with tinned chickpeas or butter beans. You can also use thin strips of belly pork instead of the sausages; you'll need about 450g.

Sweetcorn with tomato, halloumi and smoked chilli

Corn-on-the-cob is one of the nicest things to eat. I still remember smearing butter all over steaming corn cobs as a kid, and the juices running down my chin. This is now my favourite way of preparing this late summer treat. As always with veg, it's worth sourcing locally grown sweetcorn as its flavour diminishes with time and travel.

Serves 4

4 corn-on-the-cobs, husk removed
225g halloumi, cut into 1cm slices
3 tbsp extra virgin olive oil
3 garlic cloves, finely chopped
8 large ripe tomatoes, quartered
400g tin butter beans, drained
1 tbsp dried chipotle chilli flakes
A small bunch of tarragon, leaves
    picked and finely chopped
Finely grated zest and juice
    of 1 orange
20–25 ripe cherry tomatoes
    on-the-vine
A handful of flat-leaf parsley,
    leaves picked and roughly
    chopped
Sea salt and freshly cracked
    black pepper

Preheat the oven to 230°C/220°C Fan/Gas 8.

Cut each sweetcorn cob into 3 equal lengths and place in a large roasting tray with the halloumi slices. Trickle over the extra virgin olive oil, rubbing it well into the corn, and season with salt and pepper. Place in the oven for 10 minutes, turning halfway through.

Take out the roasting tray and turn the oven down to 220°C/200°C Fan/Gas 7. Add the garlic and quartered tomatoes, butter beans, chilli flakes and tarragon. Return to the oven for a further 15 minutes.

Lift out the tray again and sprinkle the orange zest and juice over everything. Add the cherry tomatoes, still on the vine (halve any loose ones and toss into the tray). Return to the oven for 5 minutes until the skin of the cherry tomatoes just starts to split.

Sprinkle over the chopped parsley, taste to check the seasoning and adjust as necessary.

Swaps
Try using mozzarella instead of halloumi, adding it just a few minutes before the end of the cooking time.

Roast lettuce, spinach and peas with herby breadcrumbs

Lettuce is so much more than a simple salad leaf. Tight-headed lettuce roasts successfully and it's also great cooked on the barbecue. The key ingredients in this recipe – lettuce, new potatoes, peas and spinach – are in season at the same time and work so well together. It's a perfect dish for a quick dinner on an early summer's night... give it a go.

Serves 4

400g new potatoes (skin on), halved
4 tbsp cold-pressed rapeseed oil
4 Baby Gem lettuce, halved lengthways
200g spinach (tougher stalks removed and roughly chopped if using large leaf spinach)
300g freshly podded or frozen peas
200ml double cream
200ml natural yoghurt
2 tsp sumac
100g sourdough or wholemeal breadcrumbs
A small bunch of flat-leaf parsley, leaves picked and finely chopped
4 sprigs of thyme, leaves picked
A small bunch of dill, leaves picked and finely chopped
Sea salt and freshly cracked black pepper

Preheat the oven to 220°C/210°C Fan/Gas 7.

Put the new potatoes into a large roasting tray. Add half of the rapeseed oil, season with salt and pepper and toss to coat. Cook in the oven for 20 minutes.

Take out the tray, turn the potatoes and spread them out. Place the lettuce halves in the roasting tray, cut side up, nestling them in among the potatoes. Trickle the remaining oil over the lettuce and season with salt and pepper. Return to the oven for 5 minutes.

Lift out the tray and stir through half of the spinach. Return to the oven for 2–3 minutes or until the spinach is wilted down. Add the remaining spinach and repeat the process to wilt the second batch fully.

Add the peas, cream, yoghurt and sumac and stir gently. Mix the breadcrumbs with the herbs and sprinkle over the creamy mixture. Place in the oven for 5 minutes until the crumb topping is golden brown and a little crunchy.

Swaps
When in season, fresh asparagus works well in place of the peas. You'll need to add it earlier – with the first batch of spinach.

Courgettes and chickpeas with tomatoes, harissa and mozzarella

This dish stems from a particularly good crop of courgettes. My partner in crime, Hayley, is fantastic at growing courgettes and it keeps me on my toes trying to invent new ways of using them. This one is quick, easy, super-tasty and thankfully uses plenty of courgettes.

Serves 4

3 tbsp extra virgin olive oil
2 medium onions, each cut into
   6 wedges
3 garlic cloves, finely sliced
2 x 400g tins chickpeas, drained
   and rinsed
4 medium courgettes, trimmed and
   cut on an angle into 2.5cm slices
2 tbsp harissa
1 preserved lemon, peel only,
   finely chopped
400g tin chopped tomatoes
2 tbsp tomato purée
2 x 125g balls of mozzarella,
   drained
A small bunch of chives, finely
   chopped
A small bunch of dill, sprigs picked
Sea salt and freshly cracked
   black pepper

Preheat the oven to 220°C/200°C Fan/Gas 7.

Put the extra virgin olive oil into a large roasting dish or tray, add the onion wedges and garlic and toss to coat with the oil. Cook in the oven for 20 minutes, stirring halfway through.

Take out the roasting dish and turn the oven down to 200°C/180°C Fan/Gas 6. Add the chickpeas, courgettes, harissa, preserved lemon, tinned tomatoes and tomato purée to the dish and stir gently to mix. Return to the oven and cook for about 15 minutes until the sauce is nicely thickened, stirring halfway through. Give it one last stir, then taste and season well with salt and pepper.

Slice the mozzarella and distribute over the courgette mix. Return to the oven for 5–10 minutes, until the mozzarella is melting and creamy.

Remove from the oven and scatter over the chopped herbs. Serve straight away, letting everyone help themselves from the dish.

Swaps
If you grow courgettes you'll probably end up with a marrow or two! Fortunately, diced peeled marrow works well in place of the courgettes here.

Pasta, courgettes and tomatoes with blue cheese topping

This is a version of a dish I've been cooking for a long time. It came about when we had an abundance of courgettes and tomatoes at the same time. It may seem a lot of olive oil but it all blends in and makes the sauce nice and creamy.

Serves 4

4 courgettes, trimmed and coarsely grated
10 ripe (or ideally slightly overripe) tomatoes, quartered
6 garlic cloves, roughly chopped
6 tbsp olive oil
225g dried wholemeal pasta shells or penne
2 bunches of basil, any thick stalks removed
200g blue cheese, such as Devon Blue
Sea salt and freshly cracked black pepper

Preheat the oven to 200°C/180°C Fan/Gas 6.

Put the courgettes, tomatoes, garlic and olive oil into a casserole dish, stir to mix and cook in the oven for 1 hour, stirring occasionally to stop the mixture catching around the side of the dish.

About two-thirds of the way through the oven cooking time, bring a pan of salted water to the boil. Add the pasta, bring back to the boil and cook until *al dente* (tender but firm to the bite). Drain well and set aside.

Remove the casserole from the oven, add the basil and then blitz the mixture using a hand-held stick blender, until you get a really smooth consistency. Add the pasta and stir to combine. Taste to check the seasoning, adding salt and pepper as needed.

Crumble the blue cheese over the surface and return the dish to the oven for about 5 minutes until the cheese is melted and golden. Serve piping hot.

Creamy summer veg roast

This is a bit like a fricassee, but in addition to the cream there's yoghurt to lend a little sharpness and cut through the richness. The inclusion of potatoes makes this an all-in-one meal, though I always ensure there's bread and a glass of cider to hand!

Serves 4

400g waxy new season potatoes (skin on)
3 tbsp extra virgin olive oil
2 medium courgettes, cut into 2cm pieces
150g freshly podded peas
150g sugar snap peas
150g green beans
A bunch of spring onions, trimmed and cut into 2cm lengths
3 Baby Gem lettuce, quartered lengthways
200g cherry tomatoes on-the-vine
200ml double cream (or coconut milk for a vegan option)
2 tbsp natural yoghurt (or coconut yoghurt for a vegan option)
A small glass of white wine or cider
A bunch of basil, leaves picked and roughly torn
Sea salt and freshly cracked black pepper

Preheat the oven to 220°C/200°C Fan/Gas 7.

Cut the potatoes into roughly 3cm pieces. Tip them into a roasting tray, add the extra virgin olive oil and toss to coat. Roast in the oven for 20 minutes or until the potatoes are just tender.

Take out the roasting tray and turn the oven setting up to 230°C/220°C Fan/Gas 8. Put all the vegetables into the tray, stir to mix with the potatoes and add the cherry tomatoes, still on the vine. Return to the oven to cook for 10 minutes.

Now add the cream, yoghurt and wine or cider and stir gently to mix with the veg. Return to the oven for another 10–15 minutes until the cream is thickened.

Add the basil and season with salt and pepper to taste. Gently stir, then serve, with a hunk of crusty bread on the side.

Swap
Any summer veg can be included in this roast – chunks of corn-on-the-cob are a particularly nice addition.

Roast beetroot, cumin and tomato crumble

When I was a kid, my mum used to cook us a savoury crumble full of tasty roots topped with a wonderful herby crumble. This topping is pretty close to her original but I've changed the filling to beetroot, tomato and cumin, which are brilliant together. I make this in early autumn, when beetroot and tomatoes are at their best and most plentiful.

Serves 4

For the filling
6 medium beetroot, peeled and
    quartered
1 tbsp cumin seeds
1 tsp nigella seeds
1 tsp fennel seeds
2 tbsp cold-pressed rapeseed oil
A pinch of cayenne pepper
6 large tomatoes, quartered
400ml passata
A small bunch of dill, sprigs picked
    and roughly chopped
Sea salt and freshly cracked
    black pepper

For the crumble topping
150g plain flour
150g fine wholemeal flour
75g cold butter, cubed (or coconut
    oil for a vegan option)
3 sprigs of thyme, leaves picked
    and finely chopped
1 sprig of rosemary, leaves picked
    and finely chopped
2 sprigs of sage, leaves picked
    and finely chopped
1 garlic clove, finely chopped
30g pumpkin seeds
30g sunflower seeds

Preheat the oven to 220°C/200°C Fan/Gas 7.

Put the beetroot, spice seeds and rapeseed oil into a casserole dish, toss to mix and cook in the oven for 20 minutes, stirring halfway through.

Take out the dish, add the cayenne, tomatoes, passata and chopped dill and stir well. Return to the oven and cook for a further 35 minutes or until the beetroot are cooked all the way through and the sauce is thickened around them. (The cooking time can vary quite a lot depending on the beetroot.)

In the meantime, make the crumble topping. Put the flours, butter, chopped herbs and garlic into a large bowl and rub together until the mixture just starts to clump. Stir through the pumpkin seeds, sunflower seeds and a little salt and pepper.

Take out the casserole dish and turn the oven down to 200°C/180°C Fan/Gas 6. Sprinkle the crumble evenly over the beetroot mix, being careful not to compact it down too much. Return to the oven and cook for 30–35 minutes until the crumble topping is golden brown. Serve at once, with a green salad on the side.

Swaps
Try my mum's classic with all the roots. In place of the beetroot, you'll need around 1kg mixed root veg. Instead of the passata, cook the roots in about 1 litre veg stock (which will reduce and thicken) until just tender. Top with the crumble and bake as above.

Roast mushrooms with beer and dumplings

Who doesn't love a big bowl of stew on a chilly autumn evening? Here, the initial roasting of the mushrooms and veg is really important to develop the deep flavours, so make sure your oven is nice and hot. Fortunately, like any great stew this is as good – if not better – the next day.

Serves 4

1kg mixed large flat and chestnut mushrooms
2 medium onions, finely chopped
2 garlic cloves, finely chopped
2 carrots, finely chopped
2 parsnips, finely chopped
2 celery sticks, finely chopped
3 tbsp cold-pressed rapeseed oil
3 tbsp tamari (or soy sauce)
1 tbsp dried seaweed flakes (optional)
330ml light ale, such as IPA
330ml stout
300ml hot veg stock
5 sprigs of thyme
3 bay leaves
A small bunch of flat-leaf parsley, leaves picked and finely chopped
Sea salt and freshly cracked black pepper

For the dumplings
200g self-raising wholemeal flour
100g butter, cubed
20g herbs (such as dill, chives and/ or parsley), chopped

Preheat the oven to 230°C/220°C Fan/Gas 8.

Coarsely grate 4 flat mushrooms; cut the rest into chunks. Cut the chestnut mushrooms into quarters. Place all the mushrooms in a large roasting tray with the onions, garlic, carrots, parsnips, celery and oil. Toss well to mix. Cook in the oven for about 30 minutes, stirring a few times, until the veg are softened and have taken on some colour.

Add the tamari (or soy), seaweed if using, ale, stout, veg stock and herbs. Return to the oven for 20 minutes, stirring a couple of times during cooking.

Meanwhile, make the dumplings. Put the flour, butter and herbs into a bowl with a pinch of salt and rub together until the mixture is the texture of breadcrumbs. Add 100ml water and mix to form a dough. Split into pieces and roll into balls, each the size of a golf ball.

Take the dish from the oven and sit the dumplings on top of the mushroom stew. Return to the oven and cook for about 15 minutes until the dumplings are doubled in size. You can turn the dumplings halfway through cooking if you like, but I prefer to leave them to get a little crusty on top with the juices caramelising around the sides.

Taste to check the seasoning, adding pepper and a little salt if needed. Serve with a salad on the side if you like and perhaps a glass of beer.

Swaps
If you can get hold of some wild mushrooms then throw in a couple of handfuls – the flavours will only get better.

Fennel with tomatoes, white wine and cream

My favourite way to enjoy this indulgent dish is for lunch, with a good hunk of sourdough to mop up all that creamy goodness, and perhaps a glass of wine. It is also an excellent accompaniment to fish or chicken.

Serves 2 (or 4 as a side)

3 fennel bulbs, trimmed
3 tbsp extra virgin olive oil
8 large ripe tomatoes, quartered
3 garlic cloves, finely sliced
A large glass of dry white wine
200ml double cream
A handful of basil leaves
Sea salt and freshly cracked
   black pepper

Preheat the oven to 220°C/200°C Fan/Gas 7.

Halve the fennel bulbs lengthways and then cut each half into 6 slim wedges. Place in a cast-iron frying pan or roasting tray, trickle over the extra virgin olive oil and toss to coat. Cook in the oven for 15 minutes.

Remove the pan from the oven (protecting your hand with an oven glove). Add the tomatoes, garlic, wine and cream, stir gently and then return to the oven. Cook for 20 minutes, or until the sauce is reduced and thickened to the consistency of double cream.

Once you have a thick and creamy consistency, remove from the oven. Season with salt and pepper to taste and tear the basil leaves over the surface. Serve from the pan.

Swaps
Replace the fennel with 4–5 medium leeks, trimmed and cut into 4cm thick slices.

Roast cauliflower cheese

Who doesn't love cauliflower cheese? It will happily grace any Sunday roast table. This delicious version deepens the flavour of the cauli, by roasting it first – like any brassica, this intensifies the flavours ten-fold. Once you've tried this, you won't want to go back to your old recipe!

Serves 2 (or 4 as a side)

2 medium cauliflowers
3 tbsp cold-pressed rapeseed oil
150g mature Cheddar, grated
150g smoked Cheddar, such as
    Dorset Red, grated
1 tbsp English mustard
250ml double cream
250g natural yoghurt
3 sprigs of thyme
A bunch of flat-leaf parsley, leaves
    picked and finely chopped
Sea salt and freshly cracked
    black pepper

Preheat the oven to 230°C/220°C Fan/Gas 8.

Remove the outer leaves of the cauliflower and split their thick ribs in half lengthways; set aside. Cut out the central stem from the cauliflower and break the head into florets. Chop the central stem into 2cm cubes. There should be no need to throw away any of the cauli unless there are some dodgy-looking outer leaves!

Place all of the cauliflower in a roasting tray. Trickle over the rapeseed oil and season lightly with salt and pepper. Toss together, place in the oven and cook for 10 minutes, stirring halfway through.

Take the tray from the oven and scatter the grated cheeses over the cauli. Mix the mustard, cream and yoghurt together in a jug, then pour into the tray. Add the herbs and stir everything together well. Taste the sauce and add a little extra seasoning if needed.

Return the roasting tray to the oven and cook for a further 5 minutes or until the sauce is bubbling and golden brown on top. Serve straight away.

Swaps
Purple sprouting broccoli, calabrese, kalettes and Brussels sprouts all work well in place of the cauliflower. And if you fancy a twist, throw in a handful of small or halved larger chestnut mushrooms with the cauli (or other brassica).

Roast Jerusalem artichokes with cream and cider

Like any dish featuring Jerusalem artichokes, this is a bit of a labour of love as they are arduous to peel, but it is totally worth it I promise! The crunchy breadcrumbs go some way to soaking up the lovely sauce, but have extra bread on the side to mop the juices if you're having this for lunch. If you have any leftovers, break down the artichokes with a fork and this becomes an excellent pasta sauce.

Serves 2 (or 4 as a side)

1kg Jerusalem artichokes
4 tbsp extra virgin olive oil
300ml double cream
200ml medium-dry cider
4 sprigs of thyme
A bunch of flat-leaf parsley,
     leaves picked and roughly
     chopped
A small handful of coarse
     breadcrumbs
Sea salt and freshly cracked
     black pepper

Preheat the oven to 220°C/200°C Fan/Gas 7.

Peel the Jerusalem artichokes and cut larger tubers into short lengths; leave small tubers whole. Tip them into a medium cast-iron frying pan or small roasting tray, trickle over the extra virgin olive oil and toss the artichokes to coat. Place in the oven for 10 minutes.

Take out the pan (protecting your hand with an oven glove). Add the cream, cider and herbs, stir to combine and return to the oven. Cook for a further 10–15 minutes or until the sauce is thickened to the consistency of double cream, checking and stirring every 5 minutes.

Season with salt and pepper to taste, scatter over the breadcrumbs and return to the oven for 5–10 minutes until the crumbs are nice and crunchy. Serve straight away, from the pan.

Swaps
For a slightly less rich version, leave out the cream. Instead, add a ladleful of chicken stock and a knob of butter to the pan and allow the liquid to cook down to a glaze.

4
ALL ABOUT VEG

This chapter is all about veg main courses – delicious, healthy meals, designed to make the most of seasonal ingredients at their best. In fact, all of the recipes are plant-based, dairy-free and suitable for vegans.

At River Cottage, we try to use seasonal and local fresh produce exclusively, but we use spicing inspired by cuisines from all over the world. Why not give parsnips and fennel the curry treatment (see page 103)? Or steal the spicing from merguez sausages and slather it all over cauliflower steaks (see page 109)? Or try a Mexican-inspired mole sauce with butternut squash (see page 118)? If, on the other hand, you fancy something a little more mellow, you could make our spelt pilaf (on page 113), or barley risotto (on page 117).

These are dishes that work whether you're cooking for yourself, the family, or for a gang of friends, and the great thing about their lack of meat, fish and dairy is that they are inclusive, too. I make no apologies for including much-maligned stuffed mushrooms (on page 100). They are gorgeous, and I can always find time to stuff them.

Mushrooms stuffed with celeriac, chilli and preserved lemons

Stuffed mushrooms can feel a bit retro, but with an innovative stuffing they are a fantastic meal. This filling is a beautiful combination of earthy celeriac and parsnip, aromatic alliums, chilli heat, citrus zing and fragrant tarragon. Thankfully there are no breadcrumbs involved in the stuffing to dull the flavours or make it stodgy. New potatoes with harissa and chard (on page 208) is an ideal accompaniment to these mushrooms.

Serves 4

1 medium celeriac, cut into
  2cm pieces
1 parsnip, cut into 2cm pieces
3 celery sticks, finely sliced
1 medium onion, finely chopped
2 garlic cloves, finely chopped
1 medium-hot red chilli, deseeded
  and finely chopped
½ preserved lemon, peel only,
  finely chopped
2 sprigs of tarragon, leaves picked
  and finely chopped
4 tbsp cold-pressed rapeseed oil
8 large flat mushrooms
Sea salt and freshly cracked
  black pepper

Preheat the oven to 220°C/200°C Fan/Gas 7.

For the stuffing, put the celeriac, parsnip, celery and onion into a large roasting tray. Add the garlic, chilli, preserved lemon, tarragon and 2 tbsp of the rapeseed oil. Season with salt and pepper and toss to mix. Roast in the oven for 30 minutes or until the celeriac and parsnips are fully softened, stirring well halfway through.

Take out the roasting tray and turn the oven up to 230°C/220°C Fan/Gas 8. Tip the contents of the tray into a bowl, mash roughly and taste to check the seasoning.

Place 4 flat mushrooms, cap side down, in the (now-empty) roasting tray. Trickle over 1 tbsp rapeseed oil and season lightly with salt and pepper. Spoon the celeriac mash into the mushrooms cups, dividing it evenly. Place the other mushrooms, cap side up, on top (effectively forming 4 mushroom sandwiches).

Brush the mushroom tops with the remaining 1 tbsp oil and season lightly with salt and pepper. Cook in the oven for 20–30 minutes, depending on the size of the mushrooms, until golden brown and cooked through.

Swaps
This celeriac and parsnip stuffing is excellent for other veg – try using it to stuff squash, following the technique on page 118.

Roast parsnip, leek and fennel curry

The real key to any good curry is deep complex flavours, achieved by including lots of individual spices rather than just relying on curry powder. To carry those spices, you need veg with big bold flavours – like parsnips, leek and fennel – that are not overwhelmed by the rich, spicy sauce.

Serves 4

3 parsnips, cut into 2cm pieces
1 leek, trimmed and cut into
   2cm thick slices
1 fennel bulb, cut into 2cm dice
3 medium onions, finely chopped
1 red pepper, deseeded and cut
   into 1cm strips
4 garlic cloves, finely chopped
100g fresh ginger, finely chopped
1 red chilli, deseeded and
   finely sliced
4 tbsp sunflower oil
1 tsp ground cumin
1 tsp ground turmeric
1 tsp ground coriander
2 tbsp good-quality medium-hot
   curry powder
1 tsp black onion seeds
3 tbsp tomato purée
400g tin chickpeas, drained
400g tin coconut milk
Finely grated zest and juice of
   2 limes
A handful of coriander
Sea salt and freshly cracked
   black pepper

Preheat the oven to 180°C/160°C Fan/Gas 4.

Put the parsnips, leek, fennel, onions and red pepper into a roasting dish. Add the garlic, ginger, chilli and sunflower oil. Season with salt and pepper and stir well to mix. Cook in the oven for 20 minutes, stirring halfway through.

Take out the dish and sprinkle all of the ground spices and onion seeds over the veg. Add the tomato purée, chickpeas, coconut milk and lime zest and juice. Stir well and then return to the oven for 20 minutes, stirring halfway through.

Remove from the oven and taste to check the seasoning. Scatter over the coriander and serve.

Swaps
Most robust veg can be swapped in here, but scrubbed new potatoes are particularly delicious in place of the parsnips. I also tend to chuck any leftover cooked veg from the fridge in towards the end of cooking – it's a great way to use them up.

Roast lettuce, new potato and spring onions with onion sauce

This slow-roasted onion sauce is so good and it can be used to enhance many veg. Here it brings roasted lettuce and new potatoes alive, with a little heat from the spring onions, to make a cracking all-in-one meal.

Serves 4

For the onion sauce
2 medium onions, cut into
    8 wedges
2 garlic cloves, roughly chopped
1 tbsp miso
1 tbsp tamari (or soy sauce)
3 sprigs of thyme
A small glass of white wine
3–4 tbsp sunflower oil
Sea salt and freshly cracked
    black pepper

For the sourdough croûtons
3 slices of sourdough
4 tbsp extra virgin olive oil

For the veg
500g new potatoes (skin on),
    cut into 2.5cm pieces
2 tbsp extra virgin olive oil
3 Baby Gem lettuce, quartered
    lengthways
2 bunches of spring onions,
    trimmed and cut into
    2.5cm lengths
2 tbsp capers, roughly chopped
A small bunch of flat-leaf parsley,
    leaves picked and finely chopped
A handful of chives, finely chopped

Preheat the oven to 160°C/140°C Fan/Gas 3.

To make the sauce, put the onions, garlic, miso, tamari (or soy), thyme and wine into a small roasting tray. Stir to mix then cover the tray with foil. Cook in the oven for 1½ hours until the onions are soft. Discard the thyme stalks.

Scrape the contents of the tray into a jug blender and blitz to a smooth, thick purée, adding a little water if necessary. With the motor running, trickle in the sunflower oil until the purée is pale and creamy (you may not need all of it). Season to taste and set aside (ready to reheat to serve).

For the croûtons, turn the oven up to 220°C/210°C Fan/ Gas 7. Rip the sourdough into 2–3cm pieces and place in a bowl with the extra virgin olive oil and some seasoning. Toss well then tip onto a baking tray and cook in the oven for 3–5 minutes. Turn the bread and bake for a further 3–5 minutes until golden brown and crisp. Transfer the croûtons to a wire rack lined with kitchen paper to drain.

Tip the potatoes into the roasting tray (used for the onion sauce). Add the 2 tbsp extra virgin olive oil and toss well. Roast in the oven for 25 minutes, stirring halfway through, until the potatoes are cooked. Take out the tray, add the lettuce, spring onions and some salt and pepper, and toss together. Return to the oven for 10 minutes.

Remove from the oven and toss the capers and chopped herbs through. Serve straight away, with the croûtons scattered over and the onion sauce on the side.

Swaps
Instead of the lettuce, use wedges of Savoy cabbage, but add them to the tray when you stir the potatoes halfway through roasting.

Slow-roasted peppers with courgettes, lentils and tomatoes

Not all roasting is about high temperatures. By cooking vegetables such as peppers and tomatoes low and slow you remove water and intensify their flavour to delicious effect. This is perfect on a summer's evening with a glass of white wine. It also makes a delicious pasta sauce.

Serves 4

3 red peppers
3 yellow peppers
2 medium onions, finely sliced
4 large tomatoes, quartered
200g cherry tomatoes
2 medium courgettes, trimmed
    and cut into 2cm slices
4 garlic cloves, finely sliced
1 tbsp rose harissa (optional)
100g Kalamata olives, pitted and
    roughly chopped
4 tbsp olive oil
400g tin green lentils, drained
    and rinsed
1 tbsp tomato purée
A bunch of basil, leaves picked
    and torn
Sea salt and freshly cracked
    black pepper

Preheat the oven to 150°C/130°C Fan/Gas 2.

Cut the red and yellow peppers lengthways into quarters and remove the core and seeds. Place in a roasting tray with the onions, all of the tomatoes, the courgettes, garlic, harissa, olives and olive oil. Toss to mix and then slow-roast in the oven for 2 hours or until all the veg and tomatoes are softened.

Take out the tray, add the lentils, tomato purée and basil and gently stir everything together. Season with salt and pepper to taste and return to the oven for 15 minutes.

Serve hot or at room temperature, with a good hunk of sourdough or warm focaccia on the side.

Swaps
Try substituting one of the courgettes with a small aubergine. You could also replace the onions with a thinly sliced fennel bulb.

Merguez cauliflower steaks with roasted cauliflower purée

Merguez spice works brilliantly with cauliflower and this recipe is a great way to use the whole veg. The nice, firm centre pieces are roasted as steaks, while the trim is turned into a silky, rich purée to serve on the side. Merguez spice blend is a firm favourite – for spicing meat and fish as well veg – so I always have a jar to hand in my storecupboard.

Serves 4

For the merguez spice blend
1 tbsp cumin seeds
1 tbsp coriander seeds
1 tbsp fennel seeds
1 tbsp caraway seeds
1 tbsp sweet paprika
½ tsp cayenne pepper (or more
    for extra heat)

For the cauliflower steaks
2 medium cauliflowers (with
    tight curds)
2 tbsp cold-pressed rapeseed oil
2 garlic cloves, finely chopped
Finely grated zest and juice of
    2 lemons
Finely grated zest and juice of
    1 orange
A small bunch of coriander,
    roughly chopped
2 sprigs of mint, leaves picked
    and finely chopped
Sea salt and freshly cracked
    black pepper

For the cauliflower purée
Trimmings from the cauliflower
1 tbsp cold-pressed rapeseed oil
2–4 tbsp sunflower oil

Preheat the oven to 200°C/180°C Fan/Gas 6.

First make the spice blend. Scatter the whole seeds on a baking tray and roast in the oven for 5 minutes or until fragrant. Take out the tray and let the toasted spice seeds cool slightly, then grind using a pestle and mortar, keeping some texture. Mix with the paprika, cayenne and a little black pepper.

Turn the oven up to 220°C/200°C Fan/Gas 7.

Remove the outer leaves from the cauliflower (if these are in good condition they can be wilted down and served with the steaks). Cut two 3cm thick slices from the centre of each cauliflower; save the trimmings.

Place these 4 cauliflower steaks in a shallow dish. Rub them with the rapeseed oil, garlic, citrus zest and plenty of the spice blend (about 1 tbsp per steak), making sure you get the flavourings into the gaps in the cauliflower; set aside. (Keep the rest of the spice blend in a sealed jar to use for seasoning other veg, meat and fish.)

To make the cauliflower purée, break up the trimmings into small florets and place in a roasting tray. Trickle over the rapeseed oil and toss together. Add 2 tbsp water to the tray and cook in the oven for 10–15 minutes until the cauliflower is completely soft.

Remove the tray from the oven and let the roasted trimmings cool slightly, for a minute or two.

continued overleaf

Tip the roasted cauliflower into a jug blender and pour on enough boiling water from the kettle to just cover it. Blitz on maximum speed, slowly trickling in the sunflower oil until the purée is pale and creamy (you may not need all of the oil, it depends on the amount of cauli trim). Season with salt and pepper to taste and set aside. (The purée can be reheated in a pan to serve.)

Turn the oven up to 220°C/210°C Fan/Gas 7.

Place the cauliflower steaks in the roasting tray (used for the trimmings) and season both sides with salt and pepper. Roast in the oven for 10–15 minutes, turning halfway through, until the cauliflower is just starting to soften in the centre stalk. It should have a good colour, even a few charred bits. Sprinkle over the citrus juices and chopped herbs and serve with the cauliflower purée on the side.

Swaps
Try using celeriac in place of cauliflower – for both the steaks and the trim for the purée.

Spelt, kimchi and apple pilaf with mangetout and green beans

This take on a rice pilaf uses spelt – a lovely ancient grain that's grown here in the UK and is much easier to digest than its more modern counterpart, wheat. The delicious grain dish is freshened with lots of crunchy peas and beans and the spicy kimchi lifts it to another level.

Serves 4–6

1 medium onion, finely chopped
1 medium carrot, finely chopped
2 celery sticks, finely chopped
¼ fennel bulb, finely chopped
2 tbsp cold-pressed rapeseed oil
300g pearled spelt, pre-soaked
    for at least 1 hour
750ml veg stock
150g mangetout, halved on
    an angle
150g green beans, trimmed
2 crisp eating apples, such as
    Cox's or Gala
200g kimchi, finely chopped
A small bunch of flat-leaf parsley,
    leaves picked and finely chopped
Sea salt and freshly cracked
    black pepper

Preheat the oven to 200°C/180°C Fan/Gas 6.

Put the onion, carrot, celery, fennel and rapeseed oil into a casserole dish. Mix well and cook in the oven (without the lid) for 20 minutes, stirring halfway through.

Drain the spelt and rinse it well. Remove the casserole from the oven, add the spelt with the veg stock and stir. Put the lid on and return to the oven for 35–50 minutes or until the spelt is cooked, stirring regularly.

Take the casserole from the oven and add the mangetout and beans. Stir to mix, put the lid back on and leave to stand for a few minutes, to allow the mangetout and beans to warm through and soften just a little in the residual heat.

Meanwhile, quarter, core and finely chop the apples. Add to the casserole with the chopped kimchi and parsley, stir through and season with salt and pepper to taste.

This can be eaten straight away but it's also delicious at room temperature, or even cold in your lunchbox the next day.

Swaps
Any crisp green veg can be introduced in place of the mangetout and/or green beans – asparagus and sugar snaps for example – it's the crunch that's important.

Spicy roast squash, onions and butter beans

Rich with coconut and sweet from the squash, this is a bit like a korma, but if you'd prefer to up the heat it will happily take an extra hit of chilli. Any leftovers will make a great lunch the next day – either hot or cold.

Serves 4

1.2kg squash, such as Crown Prince or butternut, peeled and deseeded
3 medium onions, quartered
4 garlic cloves
2 x 400g tins butter beans, drained and rinsed
2 red peppers, cored, deseeded and quartered
3 tbsp cold-pressed rapeseed oil
2 tbsp good-quality medium-hot curry powder
2 x 400ml tins coconut milk
1 tbsp tomato purée
Finely grated zest and juice of 2 limes
Sea salt and freshly cracked black pepper
A handful of coriander, chopped, to finish

Preheat the oven to 220°C/210°C Fan/Gas 7.

Cut the squash into large chunks and place in a cast-iron pan or casserole dish with the quartered onions, whole peeled garlic cloves, butter beans, red peppers and rapeseed oil. Toss well to mix and then cook in the oven for 15 minutes.

Lift out the pan, stir through the curry powder and then return to the oven. Cook for 15 minutes, stirring halfway through, until the veg are starting to soften.

Take out the pan again and stir through the coconut milk and tomato purée. Return to the oven for 15 minutes until the coconut milk is starting to thicken.

Remove from the oven and stir in the lime zest and juice. Season with salt and pepper to taste and scatter over the chopped coriander to serve.

Swaps

Chickpeas are a great alternative to the butter beans. And cauliflower works well as a swap for the squash: toss it in with the onions, butter beans and peppers about 10 minutes into the cooking rather than add it at the start, as it takes less time to cook.

Roast mushroom and chestnut barley risotto

At River Cottage, we've been making risotto with barley instead of rice for a long time. UK-grown barley is a satisfying replacement for imported rice and it's much more forgiving to cook, too. Any leftovers can be turned into arancini: blitz a small amount of the leftover barley and combine it with the rest of the mix to bind it, then shape into balls and fry until golden.

Serves 4

6 large flat mushrooms, cut into
   2cm thick slices
8–10 chestnut mushrooms, sliced
1 medium onion, finely diced
3 garlic cloves, finely chopped
3 sprigs of thyme
4 tbsp olive oil
300g pearled barley or spelt,
   pre-soaked for at least 1 hour
750ml veg stock
A glass of dry white wine
100g cooked chestnuts,
   roughly chopped
150g unsweetened chestnut purée
A small bunch of flat-leaf parsley,
   leaves picked and chopped
Sea salt and freshly cracked
   black pepper

Preheat the oven to 220°C/200°C Fan/Gas 7.

Put all the mushrooms, the onion, garlic and thyme into a casserole dish and trickle over 2 tbsp of the olive oil. Toss to mix and cook in the oven (without the lid) for 20 minutes, stirring halfway through.

Drain the barley and give it a quick rinse. Add to the casserole dish with the veg stock, wine, chestnuts and some salt and pepper. Stir well and put the lid on.

Return to the oven for 35–45 minutes, until the barley is cooked and has soaked up almost all of the liquid, stirring halfway through. If it isn't tender, add a little more stock and return to the oven. If it is cooked but still very wet remove the lid and return to the oven, stirring every 5 minutes until the liquid is just coating the barley.

Remove from the oven and stir through the remaining olive oil, the chestnut purée and most of the chopped parsley. Stir well – the chestnut purée should thicken any liquid to coat the barley. Taste to check the seasoning and pick out the thyme stalks. Scatter over the remaining chopped parsley to serve.

Swaps
You can introduce almost any veg into this risotto, but my particular favourites (other than mushrooms) are caramelised onions and leeks.

Stuffed squash and bean mole

Don't stress, no moles are involved here! Mole is a traditional sauce made with chocolate and nuts or seeds and this lovely version is full of beans. Here, I'm stuffing a squash with the mole, but it's just as good served on its own with plenty of grated cheese. If you can source one of the more unusual varieties of squash for this centrepiece, so much the better.

Serves 6

1 medium-large Crown Prince or other similar-sized squash, or 6 small butternut squash
1 tbsp cold-pressed rapeseed oil
400g peeled squash (from the neck if using butternuts), deseeded and cut into 2cm cubes
300g Jerusalem artichokes, peeled and cut into 2cm cubes
2 medium carrots, cut into 1.5cm cubes
1 medium onion, diced
4 garlic cloves, sliced
1 medium-hot red chilli, sliced (seeds retained)
3 tbsp extra virgin olive oil
400g tin chopped tomatoes
150g pumpkin seed butter (peanut works just as well)
4 tsp paprika
3 tsp ground cumin
400g tin kidney beans, drained and rinsed
400g tin butter beans, drained and rinsed
400g tin black beans, drained and rinsed
150g dark chocolate (at least 70% cocoa solids), finely chopped
Sea salt and cracked black pepper

Preheat the oven to 220°C/200°C Fan/Gas 7.

If you're using a big squash, carefully remove the top; If using portion-sized butternuts, remove and reserve the neck part. Scoop out all of the seeds, fibres and loose flesh from the squash. Brush the inside with the rapeseed oil and season with salt and pepper. Sit on a roasting tray, with the lid placed to one side if using a big squash.

Roast in the oven for 45–60 minutes depending on the size and thickness of the squash, removing the lid halfway through, if roasting, as it will cook a lot more quickly.

Put the diced squash into a separate roasting dish with the artichokes, carrots, onion, garlic, chilli and extra virgin olive oil, toss together and cook in the oven (on a shelf below the whole squash) for 30 minutes.

Meanwhile, in a bowl, whisk the tomatoes, pumpkin seed butter, paprika and cumin together. Take out the tray of roasted diced veg, pour on the tomato mixture, add all of the beans and stir well. Return to the oven for 10 minutes, then remove and stir through the chocolate until melted. Season the mole sauce with salt and pepper to taste.

Once the hollowed-out squash(es) are cooked, remove from the oven. Spoon the mole into the squash(es). Pop the lid on the big squash and serve as a stunning centrepiece, slicing a generous wedge for each of your guests and spooning plenty of mole over. Present the stuffed butternuts on individual plates. I serve an extra bowl of the mole on the side so everyone gets plenty!

Cabbage leaves stuffed with spicy nutty quinoa

Nutrient-rich quinoa has long been a staple food in South America and it's become popular in this country over the past decade or so. Fortunately, there's plenty grown in the UK these days. I like to serve these delicious cabbage parcels with the roasted cauliflower purée on page 109.

Serves 4

1 tsp cumin seeds
1 tsp coriander seeds
1 tsp fennel seeds
50g almonds (skin on),
    roughly chopped
50g hazelnuts (skin on),
    roughly chopped
50g walnuts, roughly chopped
1 medium-hot red chilli, deseeded
    and finely chopped
200g quinoa
600ml veg stock
1 medium Savoy cabbage,
    stalk removed
3 tbsp cold-pressed rapeseed oil
50g flat-leaf parsley, leaves
    picked and roughly chopped
200g baby leaf spinach
Juice of 2 lemons
Sea salt and freshly cracked
    black pepper

Preheat the oven to 200°C/180°C Fan/Gas 6. Scatter the spice seeds on a baking tray and toast in the oven for 5 minutes, or until fragrant. Let cool slightly, then roughly bash using a pestle and mortar; set aside. Now spread the nuts out on the baking tray and toast in the oven for 5–7 minutes or until lightly coloured, then remove.

Put the seeds, nuts, chilli, quinoa and veg stock into a casserole dish and mix well. Put the lid on and cook in the oven for 30 minutes, or until the quinoa is puffed up and it has absorbed all of the liquid, stirring halfway through.

Meanwhile, put the kettle on. Carefully pull away the 12 largest leaves from the cabbage and remove their hard, central rib. (Keep the rest of the cabbage for another meal or shred and sauté to serve with the parcels.) Place the cabbage leaves in a heatproof bowl, pour on enough boiling water from the kettle to cover them and leave for 7–8 minutes until pliable enough to roll. Drain and pat dry.

Take the casserole from the oven and turn the setting up to 220°C/200°C Fan/Gas 7. Add 2 tbsp of the rapeseed oil, the chopped parsley and a handful of the spinach and stir – the spinach should wilt in the residual heat. Repeat until all the spinach is added and fully wilted. Stir in the lemon juice and season with salt and pepper to taste.

Lay the cabbage leaves out flat, season and spoon some quinoa stuffing into the middle of each one. Wrap the leaves around the stuffing to enclose it. Place seam side down in a shallow roasting tray, brush with 1 tbsp oil and season. Roast for 10 minutes until the leaves are lightly coloured and a little crispy.

Roast veg 'hotpot'

This is the full veg version of a meaty hotpot. Using miso and tamari (or soy) in conjunction with the mushrooms gives a wonderful depth of flavour, which is further enhanced if you throw in some dried seaweed. The lovely sweet potato topping helps to balance out the richness.

Serves 6–8

1 medium swede
3 medium carrots
2 medium onions
200g Jerusalem artichokes
2 leeks, trimmed and cut into
    2cm slices
200g chestnut mushrooms, halved
3 garlic cloves, finely sliced
2 tbsp capers, roughly chopped
3 tbsp cold-pressed rapeseed oil
400ml passata
1 tbsp white miso
1 tbsp tamari (or soy sauce)
1 tbsp dried seaweed flakes
    (optional)
2 medium sweet potatoes, peeled
    and finely sliced
3 sprigs of thyme
Sea salt and freshly cracked
    black pepper

Preheat the oven to 200°C/180°C Fan/Gas 6.

Peel the swede, carrots and onions, cut into 1cm pieces and place in a roasting pan. Peel the artichokes, cut into 2cm pieces and add to the pan with the leeks.

Add the mushrooms, garlic and capers, trickle over 2 tbsp of the rapeseed oil and toss to mix. Roast in the oven for 40 minutes, stirring halfway through.

Add the passata, miso, tamari (or soy), and seaweed if using. Stir and return to the oven for a further 15 minutes until the sauce is thickened. In the meantime, peel and finely slice the sweet potatoes.

Remove the pan from the oven and season the mixture with salt and pepper to taste, but go easy on the salt as the miso, soy and seaweed all contribute some.

Carefully layer the sweet potato slices evenly over the surface. Brush with the remaining 1 tbsp oil, season with salt and pepper and scatter over the thyme. Return to the oven for 35–40 minutes until the sweet potatoes are cooked and crispy at the edges. Serve from the dish.

Swaps
Chunks of celeriac work very nicely in place of the Jerusalem artichokes.

5
SUNDAY ROAST

A Sunday roast is an integral part of our lives. It's a great tradition, bringing family and friends together week after week. It doesn't have to be centred around a joint, it's more about the occasion, but if you do want to cook meat the quality really does matter. At the farm we rear our own organic meat and we have a network of other organic producers to fill any gaps.

Good-quality meat will cost more, but you can stretch it by making great meals from the leftovers, or opt for cheaper cuts such as lamb breast (try the recipe on page 140). Of course, you can have a meat-free Sunday roast, and we often do. I love Stuffed marrow with tomato, chilli and basil (page 147) and Roast cauliflower with spiced yoghurt and preserved lemon (page 155) just as much as I do Butter chicken with lemon and thyme (page 126). And my Onions stuffed with roast squash, hazelnuts and chilli (page 153) can be a lovely centrepiece.

When we roast meat, it's not just a case of slamming it in the oven and forgetting about it. It's about optimising the final result. I roast flavouring ingredients with the meat which become a side dish, sauce or gravy, as for my Roast rump of beef with mustardy leeks and spinach (page 134). This doesn't mean your Sunday roast needs to be time-consuming or fiddly. If you plan ahead, you could cook my Slowly-does-it pork shoulder (page 143) or Overnight beef shin (page 137) while you sleep, and wake up to the enticing aroma of a cooked Sunday lunch.

Butter chicken with lemon and thyme

Chicken is the most popular roast to enjoy on a Sunday and rightly so. Selecting a good chicken is as important to the end result as how you cook it. An organic or properly free-range bird will have had a far better life than an indoor-reared bird, and it will be much tastier and meatier. So, it should give you lots of leftovers for sandwiches, salads and a host of classic leftover dishes, which are as delightful as the original roast.

Stuffing the cavity with lemon and thyme butter helps to keep the breast moist. It also gives you lovely juices in the tray, which can either go to make a next-level gravy or be tossed through greens or potatoes.

Serves 4

1 organic or free-range chicken
    (1.5–2kg)
1 lemon, cut into 2cm cubes
A bunch of thyme
3 garlic cloves, bashed
150g unsalted butter, cut into cubes
3 carrots, halved lengthways
2 onions, quartered
4 celery sticks, cut into 4cm lengths
Sea salt and freshly cracked
    black pepper

Take the chicken out of the fridge at least 45 minutes before cooking, to bring it to room temperature.

Preheat the oven to 210°C/190°C Fan/Gas 6½. Put the lemon, thyme, garlic and butter into a bowl with a little salt and pepper and toss to combine. Put this mixture into the chicken cavity and season the outside of the bird with salt and pepper.

Put the carrots, onions and celery into a roasting dish and pour in a small cup of water. Sit the chicken, breast side down, on top of the veg. Roast for 45 minutes.

Turn the bird over, baste and return to the oven for a further 30 minutes until golden brown and cooked through. To check, pierce the thickest part of the thigh – the juices should run clear. (Also, if you 'waggle' the leg the bone should pull away easily from the flesh.)

Leave the chicken to rest in a warm place for around 20 minutes – this will give you a much juicier result. One of the best bits of this dish is the veg in the bottom of the tray. Carve the chicken and serve with a green veg and roasties (see page 158) or new potatoes on the side.

Swaps
Try swapping the chicken and lemons for duck and oranges; the duck will take a little longer.

Slow-roast duck legs with Chinese five spice

I love duck, it's so rich and indulgent, and the fragrant spicing makes this dish a real treat. Duck legs need plenty of time to tenderise, so don't rush the cooking here.

In the unlikely event you have some duck left over, you can turn it into an amazing salad for lunch the next day. Simply crisp up the duck in a hot oven and then toss through some shredded veg and bean sprouts with just a touch of hoisin sauce. To be honest, I always cook extra duck so the salad is a guarantee!

Serves 4

4 large free-range duck legs
3 medium onions, cut into
   1cm rings
2 carrots, cut on an angle into
   1cm slices
750g new potatoes (skin on),
   halved
1 tbsp Chinese five-spice powder
Sea salt and freshly cracked
   black pepper

Take the duck legs out of the fridge at least 30 minutes before cooking to bring them to room temperature. Preheat the oven to 160°C/140°C Fan/Gas 3.

Put the sliced onions, carrots and potatoes into a large roasting pan and toss to mix.

Place the duck legs in a bowl with the five-spice powder and a little salt and pepper. Tumble to coat the duck with the seasonings and then place on top of the veg. Cook in the oven for 2 hours.

Take out the pan and turn the oven up to 220°C/210°C Fan/Gas 7. Carefully lift the duck legs out and place them on a wire rack over a tray to drain off any fat, then transfer to a plate and set aside to rest in a warm place. (If there is a lot of excess fat in the pan, tip it into a small container and save for roasting potatoes another time.)

Return the veg pan to the oven and roast for 10 minutes, stirring halfway through. Remove from the oven, place the duck legs back on top and serve.

Swaps
This works really nicely with chicken legs; just reduce the cooking time by 30 minutes.

Pot-roast brisket with beer, orange and star anise

Brisket is such a lovely cut of meat to cook. Not only does it have a deep, rich flavour but also a lovely amount of fat, which keeps it moist over the lengthy cooking it needs to become tender. To help it out further, I'm pot roasting the joint, which means it is partially covered in liquid for most of the cooking, and this liquid makes a knockout gravy.

Don't discard the veg that get cooked along with the brisket. They are full of flavour and deliciously soft at the end of cooking. If you don't like mushy veg, zap them in a blender with 2 tbsp cold-pressed rapeseed oil for a silky purée to serve alongside the beef.

Serves 6–8

1 boned and rolled joint of brisket
   (1.5–2kg)
4 tbsp sunflower or light
   rapeseed oil
2 onions, quartered
3 carrots, cut into 5cm pieces
3 celery sticks, cut into 5cm slices
8 chestnut mushrooms, halved
4 garlic cloves, bashed
2 oranges, quartered
4 star anise
½ cinnamon stick
750ml light ale, such as IPA
3 tbsp tamari (or soy sauce)
4 bay leaves
2 sprigs of thyme
Sea salt and freshly cracked
   black pepper

Take the meat out of the fridge at least an hour before cooking, to bring it to room temperature.

Preheat the oven to 230°C/220°C Fan/Gas 8. Put a deep casserole dish (large enough to hold the brisket and veg) into the oven to heat up for 10 minutes.

Season the boned and rolled brisket all over with salt. Take the hot casserole out of the oven and add the oil. Carefully lower the beef into the casserole (the oil will spit) and turn it to coat the meat all over with oil.

Return the casserole to the oven and cook for 10 minutes, then take it out again and give the brisket a quarter-turn. Return to the oven and repeat every 10 minutes until the brisket is a deep brown colour on all sides.

Take out the casserole and add the onions, carrots, celery, mushrooms and garlic. Return to the oven and cook for 20 minutes, stirring halfway through, until the veg have taken on some colour.

Take the casserole out again and turn the oven down to 160°C/140°C Fan/Gas 3. Add the oranges, star anise, cinnamon, ale, tamari (or soy), bay leaves and thyme sprigs to the casserole.

continued overleaf

If necessary, top up with a little extra beer or water to ensure the brisket is at least two-thirds immersed in liquid. Put the lid on the casserole dish.

Cook in the oven for 2½–3 hours until the brisket is juicy and tender, checking occasionally during cooking that the liquor hasn't reduced down too much and adding a little water as necessary. At the end of cooking, you should have about a 5cm depth of liquor in the casserole.

Lift the beef out of the casserole onto a warmed carving plate and set aside. Remove and discard the star anise, cinnamon, bay leaves and thyme stalks from the liquor. Squeeze the juice from the oranges out with the back of a spoon and then remove and discard the skins. Taste the liquor and season accordingly, with salt and pepper.

Remove the string from the brisket and carve the beef into slices. Serve with the pot-roasted vegetables and a ladleful of the cooking liquor.

Note
I don't mind the liquor being broth-like as long as it's tasty but if you'd prefer a thicker gravy, you can make one. Simply pour some (or all) of the liquor into a saucepan and bring to the boil. Meanwhile, mix 1 tbsp cornflour with a little cold water to a smooth paste. Once the liquor is at the boil, whisk in the cornflour mix, a little at a time, until the desired consistency is reached.

Swaps
This method works beautifully with a shoulder of pork – just swap the ale for cider.

Roast rump of beef with mustardy leeks and spinach

Rump is a premium cut and this is a perfect way to showcase it. As it is expensive, I serve this up as a special treat. With a bit of notice, a good butcher should be able to get you a rump cap – it's the muscle that sits just on top of the main rump. Failing that, a nice piece of rump will do fine.

Serves 6–8

1 beef rump cap (about 1kg)
A little sunflower oil
3 leeks, trimmed and cut into
    3cm lengths
4 garlic cloves, finely sliced
4 sprigs of thyme
1 sprig of rosemary
3 tbsp Dijon mustard
200ml double cream
A glass of dry white wine
250g spinach (tougher stalks
    removed and roughly chopped
    if using large leaf spinach)
Sea salt and freshly cracked
    black pepper

Take the meat out of the fridge at least an hour before cooking, to bring it to room temperature.

Preheat the oven to 200°C/180°C Fan/Gas 6. Place a large heavy cast-iron pan over a high heat until smoking hot. Meanwhile, season the beef with salt. Trickle a little sunflower oil into the pan and then carefully add the beef. Sear until it is deep golden brown on all sides, turning as necessary. Lift out of the meat.

Lower the heat under the pan and add the leeks, garlic, thyme and rosemary. Stir and then sit the meat on top of the veg. Roast in the oven, turning the beef occasionally until it is cooked to your liking. For medium-rare (my preference) allow about 20–25 minutes. To check, insert a digital food thermometer into the centre of the meat – it should register 46°C.

Lift the beef out of the pan and place in a warmed dish. Leave to rest in a warm place for at least 15 minutes.

Add the mustard, cream and wine to the pan and stir over a medium-high heat until reduced and thickened. Add the spinach, a handful at a time, as it wilts down. Once it is all wilted, pick out the herb stalks. Stir in the beef resting juices and season with salt and pepper to taste.

Serve the beef rump sliced, with the creamy veg and roasties (on page 158) on the side.

Swaps
This works nicely with a whole chump of pork. It needs to register 58°C in the middle and will take longer to cook.

Overnight beef shin

Cooking a whole huge shin of beef on the bone may seem daunting but, trust me, it is well worth it for the incredible flavour. Ideally, you want a shin from a front leg of the cow as the meat will be more succulent. You will need a very large deep roasting tray, at least 10cm deep (if you haven't got a big enough tray, ask your butcher to cut you smaller pieces of shin on the bone).

The low, slow method results in melting tenderness while requiring zero attention. It's one of my favourite techniques – I'm cooking and I am asleep! The only issue is waking up starving to the amazing smell of the slow-roasting beef.

Serves 8–10, plus lots of leftovers

For the overnight cook
1 whole beef shin (up to 7kg),
   ideally from a front leg
20 shallots, peeled
5 carrots, halved
3 leeks, trimmed cut into
   3cm slices
5 garlic cloves, bashed
75cl bottle decent fruity red wine
A small bunch of thyme
6 bay leaves
1 tbsp yellow mustard seeds
3 litres beef stock

To finish and serve
2 tbsp sunflower oil
1 swede, cut into 1cm dice
1 celeriac, cut into 1cm dice
2 fennel bulbs, quartered
250g tomato purée
750g cherry tomatoes
A small bunch of tarragon, leaves
   picked and roughly chopped
Sea salt and freshly cracked
   black pepper

Take the meat out of the fridge around 3–4 hours before cooking, to bring it to room temperature.

Preheat the oven to 250°C/240°C Fan/Gas 10. Rearrange the oven shelves if necessary to make enough space for the beef shin.

Lay the beef shin in a large, deep roasting tray and roast for 15 minutes. Carefully take out the tray (the hot fat will start to spit). Turn the shin over and place back in the oven for 15 minutes, or until nicely coloured all over. If necessary, return to the oven until evenly browned, turning every 5 minutes. Take out the tray.

Add the shallots, carrots, leeks and garlic to the roasting tray and cook in the oven for about 20 minutes, until well coloured, checking and turning the veg every 10 minutes.

Remove the tray from the oven and turn the oven setting down to 120°C/100°C Fan/Gas ½.

Pour in the wine and add the thyme, bay leaves and mustard seeds, then pour in the beef stock. Lay a piece of baking paper over the surface and then cover the tray with foil, pressing it around the edges of the tray to seal. Cook for at least 10 hours, preferably 12.

continued overleaf

The next day, take out the tray and remove the paper and foil. The beef should be tender enough to slip off the bone.

Turn the oven back up to 220°C/210°C Fan/Gas 7 and place a roasting pan inside to heat up for 5 minutes.

Take the hot pan from the oven and add the sunflower oil. Toss in the swede, celeriac and fennel and stir to coat. Cook in the oven for 15 minutes.

Meanwhile, lift the beef shin from the tray and place in a separate dish. Take the roasting pan from the oven and scrape the rest of the contents of the beef roasting tray into it. Stir in the tomato purée and then add the cherry tomatoes and tarragon.

Return the roasting pan to the oven and cook for a further 20–30 minutes until the sauce is thickened to a rich casserole consistency. Season with salt and pepper to taste.

Now it's up to you! Either serve the beef, loud and proud, on the bone with the sumptuous sauce on the side, or rip the meat off the bone and stir it through the chunky sauce for a more guest-friendly way. Leftovers will taste just as good the next day.

Rolled lamb breast with herbs, lemon and tomatoes

An under-rated cut, lamb breast comes from the same part of the animal as belly pork, which we know and love. Cooked well, it is tasty and tender, so give it a go. You need breasts from a decent-sized animal – consider asking your butcher for hogget breasts, which will be larger and meatier.

Serves 4

2 lamb or hogget breasts
   (about 500g each)
4 ripe tomatoes, chopped into
   1cm pieces
2 tbsp tomato purée
Finely grated zest and juice of
   2 lemons
3 garlic cloves, finely chopped
A small bunch of parsley, leaves
   picked and roughly chopped
3 sprigs of mint, leaves picked
   and roughly chopped
A small bunch of coriander,
   roughly chopped
Sea salt and freshly cracked
   black pepper

Take the lamb out of the fridge around 30 minutes before cooking, to bring it to room temperature.

Preheat the oven to 230°C/220°C Fan/Gas 8. Put the tomatoes, tomato purée, lemon zest and juice, garlic and herbs into a bowl, mix together well and season with salt and pepper.

Lay the lamb breast out flat, flesh side up, on a clean surface. Smear the tomato mixture evenly all over the surface to cover generously. Starting from a short side, roll up the lamb to form a fat roll. Tie securely with butcher's string every 2–3cm, then season the outside with salt and pepper.

Place the rolled lamb breast in a roasting tray and roast in the oven for about 30 minutes until deep golden brown on the outside. Add a glass of water to the tray and lower the oven to 170°C/150°C Fan/Gas 3. Roast the lamb for a further 2 hours until the meat is tender.

Now turn the oven up to 230°C/220°C Fan/Gas 8 for 15 minutes to crisp up the outside of the lamb.

Take the tray from the oven and leave the lamb to rest in a warm place for 5–10 minutes, then remove the string and carve into slices. I like to serve it with Five-root bash (page 207) and/or Roast purple sprouting broccoli with kimchi butter (page 175).

Swaps
For something a bit different, try stuffing the lamb with a mixture of black pudding and gooseberries.

Slowly-does-it pork shoulder

Pork shoulder is one of the most forgiving joints of meat to cook and also one of the most delicious. This all stems from the fat content bound into the muscles – even the leanest of pigs will have around 20% fat to muscle in the shoulder. For this Sunday centrepiece you need a really special piece of pork from a good fatty pig. This is another roast that I cook overnight. It will feed many people and give you lots of delicious leftovers.

Serves up to 20

1 whole pork shoulder on the bone
   (about 5kg)
3 garlic cloves
60g fresh ginger
1 red chilli, stem removed
Grated zest of 3 lemons
1 tbsp ground fennel
1 tbsp ground coriander
1 tbsp ground cumin
1 tbsp ground caraway
3 tbsp sunflower or light
   rapeseed oil
Sea salt and freshly cracked
   black pepper

Take the meat out of the fridge at least a couple of hours before cooking, to bring it to room temperature.

Preheat the oven to 230°C/220°C Fan/Gas 8. Score the skin of the pork with a Stanley knife in parallel lines, 1cm apart to a depth of 1cm.

Place the pork shoulder on a rack set in a roasting tray (to allow the fat to melt out into the tray). Roast in the oven for 20 minutes until the skin starts to crackle.

Meanwhile, put the peeled garlic and ginger into a food processor with the chilli, lemon zest, ground spices and oil. Blitz to a paste, adding a little water to loosen the mixture if necessary.

Remove the pork from the oven and spread the spice paste all over the surface. Add a glass of water to the roasting tray and return to the oven. Turn the oven setting down to 120°C/100°C Fan/Gas ½ and cook for 12–14 hours (ideally overnight while you sleep).

Remove the pork from the oven and leave to rest in a warm place for at least an hour. To serve, remove the skin crackling and break it up into pieces. Roughly shred the meat and serve on a warmed platter with the crackling.

Swaps
A whole lamb shoulder is also delicious cooked this way. It will need a lot less cooking – a maximum of 8 hours depending on the size.

Whole roast flat fish with green beans and tomatoes

This is a wonderful way to cook flat fish. For a celebration, I choose turbot, 'the king of fish', which is caught around the British isles. It has a majestic flavour and texture with a price to match, but this recipe also works well with smaller, less expensive fish such as brill, or even a good-sized plaice. If you can only get one-portion-sized fish, you can squeeze several into the tray as long as the fattest parts of the fish don't overlap.

As the fish roasts, the juices released by the tomatoes and fish mingle with the olive oil to delicious effect, so be sure to spoon some of that juice over the fish before you tuck in.

Serves 4–8 depending on the fish

1 turbot (ideally 2–2.5kg) or other flat fish (see above)
4 tbsp extra virgin olive oil
1kg mixed heritage tomatoes (a variety of sizes)
400g green beans (ideally assorted colours), trimmed
4 garlic cloves, thinly sliced
Sea salt and freshly cracked black pepper

Preheat the oven to 200°C/180°C Fan/Gas 6.

Lay the fish flat in a large roasting tray. Trickle over half of the extra virgin olive oil and rub all over the fish. Season on both sides with salt and pepper.

Halve or quarter the larger tomatoes. In a large bowl, gently toss all the tomatoes with the green beans, sliced garlic, remaining 2 tbsp oil and some seasoning. Scatter the mixture around the fish.

Place in the oven and roast, allowing about 25 minutes for a 2–2.5kg fish, or 10–15 minutes for a smaller 1–1.5 kg fish. To check the fish is cooked, pierce the fattest part near the middle: the flesh should have just changed colour and become tender through to the bone. If not, then return to the oven to finish cooking, checking every 3–4 minutes. Don't overcook it!

Serve the fish and veg straight from the tray, with plenty of crusty bread on the side to mop up the delicious juices.

Swaps
Try using wedges of fennel instead of the beans, and when broad beans are in season a scattering won't goes amiss. Instead of whole fish, you can cook fish portions this way. Use the thickest pieces you can find, at least 3cm thick, so they cook in the same time as the veg.

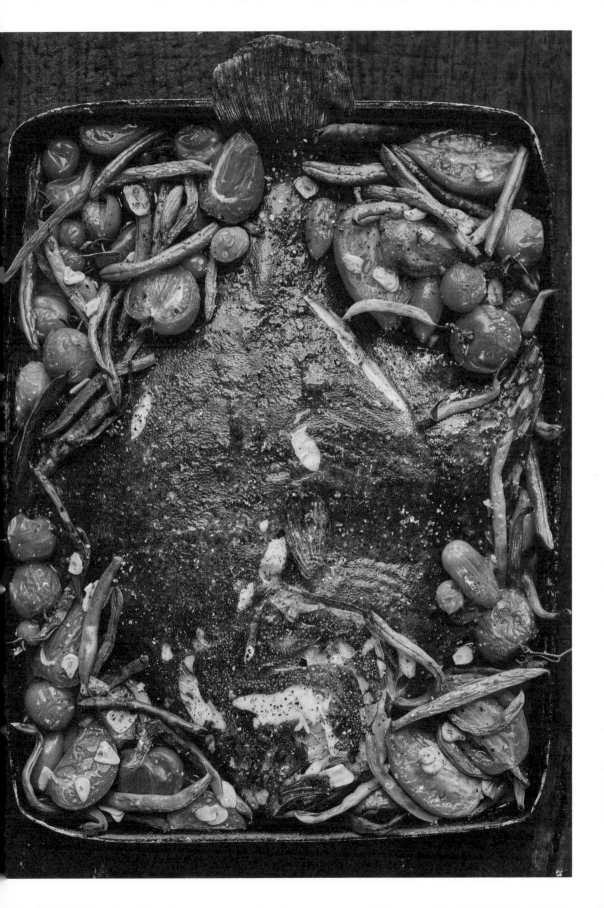

Stuffed marrow with tomato, chilli and basil

If you grow courgettes in the garden, as I do, it's inevitable that you'll miss picking the odd one at the right time and end up with a few marrows. They have a reputation for being tasteless but a marrow can be wonderful if you roast or pan-fry it. The key is to avoid cooking this veg in water, which dilutes the flavour and ruins the texture.

This is a showstopper way to stuff a marrow. The filling is incredibly tasty – it also makes an excellent one-tray roast: just keep it in the pan (or a roasting dish), slice over some mozzarella and return to the oven to melt.

Serves 4

1 medium-large marrow
  (at least 1kg), or other
  similar-sized summer squash
4 tbsp extra virgin olive oil
1 medium onion, chopped
2 garlic cloves, chopped
1 tsp paprika
100g sun-dried tomatoes,
  roughly chopped
½ medium-hot red chilli (or more
  for extra heat), deseeded and
  finely chopped
½ preserved lemon, peel only,
  finely chopped
400g tin chopped tomatoes
1 tbsp tomato purée
A bunch of basil, leaves picked
  and torn
Sea salt and freshly cracked
  black pepper

Preheat the oven to 230°C/220°C Fan/Gas 8.

Cut the marrow in half lengthways – this can be tricky as the skin tends to be tough, so take care. Scoop out the seeds with a spoon and discard (or dry them and save to plant and grow next year). Score the inside of the deepest marrow half, cutting at least 5mm deep but being careful not to cut through the skin. Set the other half aside.

Rub the inside of the scored marrow with 2 tbsp of the extra virgin olive oil and season well with salt and pepper. Place, cut side up, in a shallow roasting tray and roast in the oven for 25–35 minutes, depending on the size of the marrow, until tender. It should take on some colour around the edge, and may release some liquid into the cavity (if so, save this to use later on).

While the marrow is roasting, deseed and peel the other half and cut into 2cm chunks, Place a heavy cast-iron pan over a high heat. Once it is hot, add the remaining 2 tbsp oil and toss in the marrow cubes. Cook over the high heat, turning occasionally, until coloured on all sides.

Lower the heat slightly under the pan and add the onion and garlic. Cook for around 5 minutes until the onion is starting to soften.

continued overleaf

Add the paprika, sun-dried tomatoes, chilli, preserved lemon and tinned tomatoes. Stir well and place the pan in the oven (with the roasting marrow). Cook for 10 minutes.

Check the roasting marrow half: if there is any liquid in the cavity, tip it into the pan and stir through the filling, along with the tomato purée and basil leaves. Return to the oven for 5 minutes. Take out the pan and give the filling another stir. It should be nicely thickened now; if not return to the oven for another 5 minutes or so.

Once cooked, remove the marrow from the oven and carefully spoon the filling into the cavity. Return to the oven and cook for 10 minutes until the filling starts to brown on top.

Serve the stuffed marrow hot. If you have any stuffing left over, it makes an excellent sauce for pasta or gnocchi.

Swaps
Downsize the marrow to courgettes and bake the halves for just 20 minutes before adding the stuffing.

Mum's nut roast

Nut roast is something of a joke among vegetarians, as it is considered a lazy alternative to a meat roast and is often nothing more than a stuffing recipe with nuts thrown into the mix. For a different-level nut roast, try this version. I've been eating it for as long as I can remember. It's simply delicious, still a family favourite and is connected to so many happy memories for me that I had to share it with you... with my mum's permission, obviously! I hope you enjoy it as much as the Alderson clan has over the years.

Serves 4

75g pumpkin seeds
150g almonds (skin on),
    roughly chopped
75g cashew nuts, roughly chopped
75g hazelnuts, roughly chopped
2 medium onions, finely chopped
2 garlic cloves, chopped
2 celery sticks, finely chopped
150g chestnut mushrooms, grated
3 sprigs of thyme, leaves picked
2 sprigs of sage, leaves picked
    and finely chopped
2 tbsp extra virgin olive oil
100g fresh breadcrumbs
200g cooked chestnuts,
    roughly chopped
200g chestnut purée
1 tablespoon tamari (or soy sauce)
100ml veg stock
Sea salt and freshly cracked
    black pepper

Preheat the oven to 200°C/180°C Fan/Gas 6.

Roughly bash the pumpkin seeds, using a pestle and mortar. Tip the almonds, cashews, hazelnuts and bashed pumpkin seeds onto a baking tray and toast in the oven for 5 minutes. Tip onto a plate and set aside.

In a roasting dish, measuring about 25 x 20cm, combine the onions, garlic, celery, mushrooms, thyme, sage and extra virgin olive oil. Toss well and cook in the oven for 20 minutes, stirring halfway through.

Take the dish from the oven and add the toasted nut and seed mix, breadcrumbs, chopped chestnuts, chestnut purée, tamari (or soy) and veg stock. Mix thoroughly, then taste and season accordingly with salt and pepper. Press the mixture into the dish, with the back of a spoon.

Return to the oven and cook for 30 minutes, until the nut roast is crisp and golden brown on top. Serve with cabbage or other seasonal green veg.

Onions stuffed with roast squash, hazelnuts and chilli

This is a version of a dish we served to 470 guests at a charity vegan banquet at The Savoy, to raise funds for Compassion in World Farming. It's simple to put together, yet stunning to look at and the stuffing is full of sweet, spicy, earthy flavours. It certainly deserves a place at the top table. Savoy cabbage with apples, parsley and chestnuts (page 172) and Roast five-root bash (page 207) are perfect accompaniments.

Serves 4

8 medium white onions
A glass of white wine
3 sprigs of thyme
400g squash, such as Crown Prince
  or butternut, peeled, deseeded
  and cut into 2.5cm pieces
50g hazelnuts, roughly chopped
1 red chilli, deseeded and
  finely chopped
Finely grated zest and juice of
  1 orange
Finely grated zest and juice of
  1 lime
3 tbsp extra virgin olive oil
2 tbsp sunflower oil
Sea salt and freshly cracked
  black pepper

Preheat the oven to 180°C/160°C Fan/Gas 4.

Remove the outermost layer, as well as the papery skin from the onions then place, root side down, in a small roasting tray. Add the wine and thyme sprigs, cover the tray with foil and cook in the oven for 1 hour, or until soft.

Meanwhile, put the squash into a small roasting dish with the hazelnuts, chilli, citrus zest, 2 tbsp of the olive oil and some seasoning. Toss to mix and roast for 20–30 minutes until softened. Take the dish from the oven, add the citrus juice and roughly mash with a fork. Check the seasoning.

Once the onions are cooked, take them out and turn the oven up to 230°C/220°C Fan/Gas 8. When the onions are cool enough to handle, carefully cut away the root end and gently tease out the centres, leaving the two outer layers intact; keep the prised-out onion flesh. Now gently push the squash mixture into the onion cavities, so they look like whole onions again.

Return the stuffed onions to the roasting tray, brush with the remaining olive oil and season with salt and pepper. Cook in the oven for 15–20 minutes until the filling is piping hot and the onions gain a little colour.

Meanwhile, blitz the soft onion flesh in a jug blender, then slowly trickle in the sunflower oil to make a creamy sauce. Check the seasoning and reheat if necessary to serve.

Serve the stuffed onions with the sauce poured over.

Roast cauliflower with spiced yoghurt and preserved lemon

As a child I couldn't stand cauliflower in any form, but over the years my feelings have changed and I've grown to love this mighty brassica. I have created many a recipe to enjoy it and this is my favourite 'show off' dish. It looks so grand as you bring it to the table, truly deserving to be the centre of attention.

Serves 4

1 tsp cumin seeds
1 tsp coriander seeds
1 tsp caraway seeds
1 tsp fennel seeds
1 tsp yellow mustard seeds
1 tsp fenugreek
1 tsp ground cardamom
1 tsp ground cinnamon
2 tsp paprika
50g fresh ginger, peeled
4 garlic cloves, peeled
3 pieces of fresh turmeric root,
   peeled (or 1 tsp ground)
200g natural yoghurt
1 medium cauliflower (800g–1kg),
   ideally with lots of good outer
   leaves
½ hispi cabbage or ½ bunch of
   spring greens, divided into leaves
1 preserved lemon, peel only,
   finely sliced
3 tbsp cold-pressed rapeseed oil
4 sprigs of mint, leaves picked
   and roughly torn
Sea salt and freshly cracked
   black pepper

Preheat the oven to 200°C/180°C Fan/Gas 6.

Put all of the seeds and the fenugreek into a roasting pan or tray (you may as well use the same one to roast the cauli in so make sure it is 5–7cm deep). Toast in the oven for 5 minutes, then check and stir. Return to the oven for a further 2–3 minutes until fragrant and evenly coloured, but be careful not to burn the spices as they'll be really bitter if you do. Remove from the oven and allow to cool.

Either blitz the toasted spice seed mix in a spice grinder or grind using a pestle and mortar to a fine powder. Transfer to a medium bowl and add the cardamom, cinnamon and paprika.

Now put the ginger, garlic, and fresh turmeric if using, into the spice grinder and grind to a smooth paste (or use the pestle and mortar), adding a little water if needed.

Add the yoghurt to the ground spices, along with the ginger and garlic paste (and ground turmeric if using). Stir well and season with salt and pepper to taste.

Remove the outside leaves from the cauliflower and put to one side. Tear off a large piece of baking paper (big enough to completely wrap the cauliflower).

Place the whole cauliflower in the centre of the paper. Smother it with about half of the spiced yoghurt mix and massage this into every nook and cranny.

continued overleaf

Now pour the rest of the spiced yoghurt mix over the cauliflower and bring the sides of the baking paper up around the outside of the veg. Scrunch the edges of the paper together over the top of the cauliflower and tie securely with kitchen string. Place in the roasting pan or tray and cook in the oven for 30 minutes.

Remove from the oven and pierce the centre of the cauliflower through the paper with a thin knife or skewer: you should meet just a little resistance as you reach the centre stalk of the cauliflower; if it is still a little hard, return to the oven for 10–15 minutes.

Scatter the cauliflower leaves, cabbage and preserved lemon slices around the cauliflower parcel. Trickle over the rapeseed oil, season with salt and pepper and cook in the oven for 10 minutes. Toss the greens and return to the oven for a further 5 minutes.

Serve from the roasting tray, releasing the paper and cutting open the cauliflower at the table for maximum effect and aroma. Scatter over the mint to garnish.

Swaps
Instead of the curry spices, try using the merguez spice blend from the recipe on page 109.

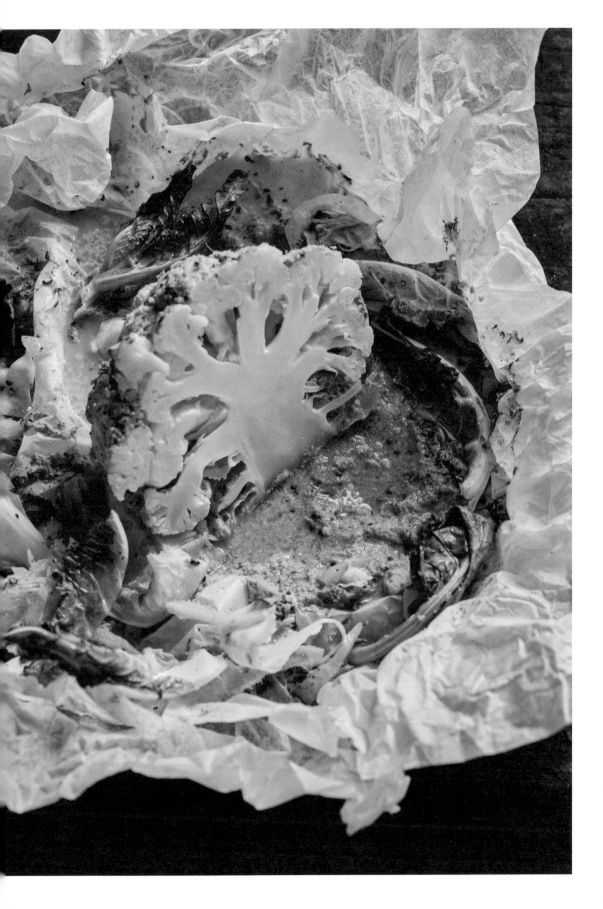

River Cottage roasties

Roast potatoes are a much-loved part of any Sunday lunch and we all have our own way of preparing them. This is the way they are roasted for Sunday lunch at River Cottage and it's my favourite. Choosing the right potato is important, so don't just settle for an 'all-rounder'. I love roasting spuds in beef dripping but a light cooking oil, such as sunflower, will yield equally delicious crispy results.

Serves 4

1kg Maris Piper or King Edward
   potatoes
150g beef dripping or sunflower oil
Sea salt and freshly cracked
   black pepper

Preheat the oven to 230°C/220°C Fan/Gas 8.

Bring a large pan of water to the boil. (You need plenty of water to ensure the potatoes come back to the boil quickly once they are added.) Peel the potatoes and cut each one into 2, 3 or 4 pieces, depending on size.

Add the potatoes to the fast-boiling water and cook for about 10 minutes, the exact time depending on the variety and time of the year. To check, lift out one of the potatoes with a slotted spoon and use a fork to scrape the outside. If the outer 2–3mm comes away like mash they are good to go. Drain and leave to steam-dry in the colander for a few minutes, then return to the (now-dry) pan. Put the lid on and shake vigorously.

Put the beef dripping or oil into a shallow metal roasting tray and place in the oven until the fat is very hot. Sprinkle the potatoes in the pan generously with salt and give them one more shuffle. Now take the tray from the oven and gently tip the potatoes into the hot fat (it is liable to spit, so take care). Turn each potato in the fat until all the sides are coated then roast in the oven for 10 minutes.

Take out the tray, turn each potato onto a different side and return to the oven for a further 10 minutes. Repeat this process until all the sides are crisp and golden. By this time, the potatoes will be beautifully cooked and fluffy in the middle. Drain them on kitchen paper or a clean cloth, then transfer to a warmed serving dish and sprinkle with salt and pepper to serve.

Foolproof Yorkshire puds

These are an essential part of any Sunday roast in my view, not just beef. Making Yorkshire puddings was one of the first things I learnt as a cook and I haven't really deviated from this recipe since. The key is to use equal volumes of the batter ingredients, so all you need is a standard (300ml) coffee mug!

I use the shallow Yorkshire trays (which normally have 4 wide, shallow cups) and cook the puds in batches. If you prefer to use a 12-cup muffin tray, extend the cooking time by 5 minutes. You can cook the Yorkshires a little ahead and pop them in the oven for a minute or two to warm through just before serving.

Makes about 12

1 mug of plain white flour, sifted
1 mug of whole milk
1 mug of eggs (about 6; crack in
    enough eggs to fill the mug)
100g beef dripping, or sunflower oil
    for a veggie option
Sea salt and freshly cracked
    black pepper

Have your Yorkshire pudding tray(s) ready. To make the batter, put the flour, milk and eggs into a bowl and whisk together briefly, just to combine. Now season with salt and pepper. Pass the batter through a sieve into a jug.

Ideally you should rest the batter for at least an hour before cooking, but if you're in a rush you can use it straight away – you'll just get Yorkshires that cook slightly more unevenly.

Preheat the oven to 220°C/210°C Fan/Gas 7. Put a rounded teaspoonful of beef dripping or 2 tsp sunflower oil into each cup in the tray(s) and place in the oven for 5 minutes or until the oil is very hot.

Take the trays from the oven and immediately ladle the batter into the cups to half-fill them. Don't be tempted to over-fill them as this will result in spongy puddings. Immediately place in the oven and cook for 15 minutes until golden brown and crispy. Do not open the door at any point during this time or they will sink.

If, after 15 minutes, the Yorkshires are not quite crisp and well coloured, cook for a further 5 minutes. Repeat until all the batter is used.

Serve piping hot, with your chosen roast and gravy.

Lancashire hotpot

My grandad was from Lancashire and I'm sure he enjoyed a hotpot many times, but sadly he's not around to share his experiences. Over the years, I've researched this classic and finally settled on my preferred recipe, which uses shoulder rather than the more traditional lamb chops. If you're able to source mutton, use it here – to take the flavour to the next level.

Serves 4

500g lamb, hogget or mutton shoulder, diced
2 lamb, hogget or mutton kidneys, quartered, tough core removed and cut into 1cm cubes
2 medium onions, diced
2 carrots, diced
1 garlic clove, finely sliced
3 tbsp sunflower oil
30g plain flour
600ml lamb stock (or you can use chicken stock)
2 sprigs of thyme
1 sprig of rosemary
2 tsp Worcestershire sauce
750g potatoes, such as Maris Piper or King Edward
Sea salt and freshly cracked black pepper

Preheat the oven to 220°C/210°C Fan/Gas 7.

Put the diced meat into a cast-iron pan or casserole dish with the kidneys, onions, carrots, garlic and sunflower oil. Toss to mix and cook in the oven for 20 minutes, stirring a few times to ensure everything takes on some colour.

Take out the pan or casserole dish and turn the oven down to 160°C/140°C Fan/Gas 3. Sprinkle in the flour and stir through the veg and meat. Pour over half of the stock, stir well and add the thyme, rosemary and Worcestershire sauce. Return to the oven and cook for 1 hour, stirring every 15 minutes or so. In the meantime, peel and finely slice the potatoes into 3mm thick slices.

Take the pan or dish out of the oven and pick out the hard thyme and rosemary stalks. Taste and season with salt and pepper accordingly. Layer the potato slices over the top of the veg and meat. Pour over the remaining stock and return to the oven for 30 minutes.

Now turn the oven up to 210°C/190°C Fan/Gas 6½ and continue to cook until the stock is reduced to below the potato topping and the potato slices are a lovely golden brown colour. This will take around 30–40 minutes.

Traditionally, Lancashire hotpot is served on its own, without accompaniments.

Swaps
Goat works well in place of mutton. And sweet potatoes for the topping – just don't tell anyone from Lancashire!

Roast chicken curry pie

Growing up in the Midlands, curry was a big thing. I'm not sure where
I had my first curry pie but it's stuck with me. The ingredients list might
be lengthy but the pie doesn't take long to put together. Serve it with
a good pile of creamy mash and you'll be in for a real treat.

Serves 4

For the pastry
300g plain white flour
40g fine wholemeal flour
A good pinch of fine sea salt
170g cold butter, cubed
2 eggs, beaten, plus an extra
    beaten egg for the egg wash
1–2 tbsp milk

For the filling
3 medium onions, finely chopped
4 garlic cloves, finely chopped
100g fresh ginger, finely chopped
1 red pepper, cored, deseeded
    and cut into 1cm strips
1 red chilli, deseeded and
    finely sliced
4 tbsp sunflower oil
400g leftover roast chicken, or
    diced fresh leg and thigh meat
1 tsp ground cumin
1 tsp ground turmeric
1 tsp ground coriander
1 tsp black onion seeds
2 tbsp medium-hot curry powder
3 tbsp tomato purée
400g tin chickpeas, drained
400g tin green lentils, drained
400g tin coconut milk
Grated zest and juice of 2 limes
Sea salt and cracked black pepper

To make the pastry, put the flours and salt into a bowl,
add the butter and rub into the flour until you have the
texture of fine breadcrumbs. Add the beaten eggs and
1 tbsp milk and mix together quickly – the pastry should
come together easily and be a bit sticky; if not add a little
extra milk. Once the pastry forms a ball, knead lightly, for
1–2 minutes. Shape into a flat disc, wrap in baking paper
and refrigerate for at least 1 hour.

Preheat the oven to 180°C/160°C Fan/Gas 4. To make
the filling, put the onions, garlic, ginger, red pepper, chilli
and sunflower oil into a large roasting tray. If using fresh
chicken, add it in now. Stir to combine and cook in the
oven for 40 minutes, stirring halfway through.

Take out the tray and add all the rest of the ingredients,
including the cooked chicken if using. Add 200ml water,
stir and return to the oven for 30 minutes, stirring halfway
through. Remove and taste to check the seasoning. Leave
to cool. Turn the oven up to 200°C/180°C Fan/Gas 6.

To assemble, roll out the pastry on a floured surface until
it is large enough to cover the roasting tray, with some
overhang. Carefully roll the pastry around the rolling
pin and unravel over the roasting tray. Press the edges
against the side of the tray and crimp them.

Brush the pastry all over with egg wash and pierce in a
few places with a knife to let the steam escape. Decorate
with leaves or other shapes (a chicken perhaps!) cut from
the pastry trimmings. Brush these with egg wash. Return
to the oven and cook for 30 minutes until the pastry is
golden brown. Serve piping hot.

Creamy fish pie

If you eat fish, you probably like fish pie – and what's not to like? This creamy version is enriched with brown crab meat, which gives it a lovely, sultry, shellfish note. The smell of this pie cooking will fill your kitchen with hungry family members, and quite possibly any close neighbours! Roast purple sprouting broccoli with kimchi butter (on page 175) is a particularly good accompaniment.

Serves 4–6

500g new potatoes, scrubbed
4 tbsp extra virgin olive oil
2 leeks, trimmed and cut into
   1cm slices
3 celery sticks, very finely sliced
200g fennel, thinly sliced
300g MSC-certified white fish,
   such as hake or pollack, skinned
   and cut into 2cm dice
200g MSC-certified smoked white
   fish, such as haddock, skinned
   and cut into 2cm dice
100g brown crab meat
10g capers, roughly chopped
A small bunch of flat-leaf parsley,
   leaves picked and roughly
   chopped
A small bunch of dill, sprigs picked
   and roughly chopped
300ml double cream
A small glass of dry white wine
200g mature Cheddar, grated
Sea salt and freshly cracked
   black pepper

Preheat the oven to 220°C/200°C Fan/Gas 7.

Place the new potatoes in a shallow roasting tray, trickle over 2 tbsp of the extra virgin olive oil and season lightly with salt and pepper. Toss to coat and roast in the top of the oven for 25–30 minutes until the potatoes are just starting to soften.

Meanwhile, put the leeks, celery and fennel into a roasting dish with the remaining 2 tbsp oil and toss to mix. Cook in the oven for 10 minutes, then take out the dish.

Add all of the fish, the brown crab meat, capers, parsley, dill, cream and white wine to the roasting dish, season with salt and pepper and stir gently to mix with the veg. Cook in the oven for 20 minutes.

Once cooked, remove the potatoes from the oven and break them apart roughly with a fork. Spoon the bashed potatoes evenly over the fish filling and scatter the grated cheese on top. Return to the oven for 5–10 minutes until the cheese is melted and starting to brown. Remove from the oven.

Serve the fish pie at once, with a green veg on the side.

Swaps
Replace the brown crab with freshly shelled mussels or MSC-certified prawns.

Mushroom, celeriac, blue cheese and chestnut pie

I love to serve up a pie on a Sunday occasionally. It makes a change from a roast and this is a great veggie meal. You can even prepare the pastry and filling the day before, ready to assemble and cook the following day. It's perfect for a winter Sunday lunch, but also for a weekday supper.

Serves 4–6

For the pastry
300g plain white flour, plus extra to dust
40g fine wholemeal flour
A good pinch of fine sea salt
170g cold butter, cubed
2 eggs, beaten, plus an extra beaten egg for the egg wash
1–2 tbsp milk

For the filling
1kg large flat mushrooms, halved
1 medium celeriac, cut into 1cm cubes
3 celery sticks, cut into 1cm pieces
4 garlic cloves, chopped
200g peeled cooked chestnuts
1 sprig of rosemary
3 tbsp extra virgin olive oil
2 glasses of full-bodied red wine
200g medium-strength blue cheese, such as Devon Blue, crumbled
150ml double cream
A small bunch of flat-leaf parsley, leaves picked and finely chopped
Sea salt and freshly cracked black pepper

To make the pastry, put the flours and salt into a bowl, add the butter and rub into the flour until you have the texture of fine breadcrumbs. Add the beaten eggs and 1 tbsp milk and mix together quickly – the pastry should come together easily and be a bit sticky; if not add a little extra milk. Once the pastry forms a ball, knead for 1–2 minutes. Shape into a flat disc, wrap in baking paper and refrigerate for at least 1 hour.

Preheat the oven to 220°C/200°C Fan/Gas 7.

To make the filling, put the mushrooms, celeriac, celery, garlic, chestnuts, rosemary and extra virgin olive oil into a roasting dish. Toss together and cook in the oven for 20 minutes, stirring halfway through.

Take out the dish and add the wine, blue cheese, cream and parsley. Stir to combine then return to the oven for 10–15 minutes until the liquor is thickened. Remove and season with salt and pepper to taste. Leave to cool.

To assemble, roll out the pastry on a lightly floured surface until large enough to cover the roasting dish with about 3cm overhanging. Lift the pastry over the top of the dish, press the edges against the rim and crimp them. Brush the pastry all over with egg wash and make 2 slits in the top with a knife to let the steam escape. Cook in the oven for about 30 minutes, until the pastry is crisp and dark golden. Serve hot, with a green veg of your choice.

Swaps
If you fancy a meatier version swap the chestnuts for pieces of homemade 'chorizo' on page 29.

6
SUPER
SIDES

Featuring vegetables in season, the mouth-watering recipes in this chapter can be used in two equally delicious ways.

You can cook one or two of the recipes to accompany something from the Sunday roast chapter (or any other main course) instead of serving up plain veg. I recommend Brussels sprouts with prunes, walnuts and clementines (page 176) with beef; Asparagus with spinach and roasted garlic butter (page 180) with chicken; and Three-root dauphinoise (page 204) with pretty much anything.

Alternatively, you can treat them more like a mezze. Cooking three or four of the recipes together not only makes a fabulous meal, but is economically efficient too, because it makes the most of the heat of your oven. In fact, this is a plus for roasting in general – the only limit to how many things you can roast at once is the number of shelves in your oven.

We love to serve up Roast tomatoes with fennel, preserved lemon and chilli (page 182), alongside Celeriac with raisins, almonds and parsley (page 193), and Carrots, honey, orange and thyme (page 190), all of which can also be turned into wonderful salads. Or, what about Roast purple sprouting broccoli with kimchi butter (page 175), partnered with Cabbage, carrots and shallots with hazelnut satay (page 188)? These assemblies are all vegetarian, too.

Savoy cabbage with apples, parsley and chestnuts

One of nature's pure beauties, both in terms of flavour and appearance, Savoy cabbage is among my favourite veg. The addition of chestnuts enhances its mildly nutty taste and the apples are a lovely fruity contrast to the brassica flavour.

Serves 4

1 Savoy cabbage
Finely grated zest and juice of
   1 lemon
3 tbsp cold-pressed rapeseed oil
2 eating apples, quartered, cored
   and sliced
150g peeled roasted chestnuts,
   broken into large pieces
A small bunch of flat-leaf parsley,
   leaves picked and roughly
   chopped
Sea salt and freshly cracked
   black pepper

Preheat the oven to 220°C/210°C Fan/Gas 7.

Cut the Savoy cabbage into 6 wedges, from the top down, keeping a little root on each wedge so they stay intact. If any leaves fall off, keep them. Rinse each cabbage wedge and allow to dry for a few minutes.

Put the cabbage wedges and any loose leaves into a roasting tray. Scatter over the lemon zest, add the rapeseed oil and season with salt and pepper. Rub into the cut surfaces of the cabbages. Cook in the oven for 5 minutes.

Lift out the tray and turn each cabbage wedge. Scatter the apples, chestnuts and parsley over the cabbage and cook in the oven for a further 10 minutes or until the cabbage is tender.

Remove the roasting tray from the oven. Taste to check the seasoning and adjust as necessary, then squeeze over the lemon juice and serve.

Roast purple sprouting broccoli with kimchi butter

I love purple sprouting. It is so much more complex than standard broccoli and it's not all about the fluffy floret – the firm stem and leaves are all part of its splendour. I always have some sort of kimchi or spicy kraut on the go, but if you're not up for fermenting yourself, buy a chilled live kimchi.

Serves 4

500g purple sprouting broccoli
150g kimchi, finely chopped
2 tbsp tamari (or soy sauce)
100g butter, softened
1 tbsp dried seaweed flakes
  (optional)
A bunch of coriander, leaves picked
  and roughly chopped
Sea salt and freshly cracked
  black pepper

Preheat the oven to 220°C/210°C Fan/Gas 7.

Don't be tempted to trim the purple sprouting too much. Just halve the bottom of each stem lengthways so the thickest part will cook in the same time as the rest.

In a bowl, mix the kimchi and tamari (or soy sauce) with the softened butter, along with the seaweed if using.

Place the purple sprouting in a roasting tray and dot with the flavoured butter. Season with salt and pepper but go easy on the salt as the kimchi (and seaweed if using) contribute a fair amount. Cook in the oven for 15 minutes or until the broccoli is tender, stirring halfway through.

Remove the roasting tray from the oven, toss through the chopped coriander and serve.

Swaps
Replace the purple sprouting with wedges of Savoy or hispi cabbage – both are lovely prepared this way.

Brussels sprouts with prunes, walnuts and clementines

This is a perfect veg dish to accompany your Christmas dinner, but Brussels sprouts are in season throughout the winter so you can enjoy them beyond the festive feast. Put aside those memories of sludgy over-boiled sprouts. Try this dish and you'll appreciate what a wonderful veg this brassica is.

Serves 4

750g Brussels sprouts, halved vertically (through the stalk)
100g walnuts, roughly chopped
4 clementines, halved horizontally
2 tbsp cold-pressed rapeseed oil
200g prunes, roughly chopped
A small bunch of flat-leaf parsley, leaves picked and roughly chopped
Sea salt and freshly cracked black pepper

Preheat the oven to 220°C/210°C Fan/Gas 7.

Put the Brussels sprouts, walnuts, halved clementines and rapeseed oil into a roasting tray, toss together and season well with salt and pepper. Cook in the oven for 10 minutes. Take out the tray, toss everything together again and return to the oven for a further 5 minutes or until the sprouts are cooked.

Remove the tray from the oven and add the prunes. Now use the back of a fork to squeeze the juice and flesh out of 2 clementine halves over the veg and fruit (do this carefully as they will be hot). Add the chopped parsley and give everything a good stir to mix.

Taste to check the seasoning and adjust as necessary, then serve. You can eat the entire clementine halves, including the skins... delicious.

Swaps
Use fresh apples or pears, quartered and cored, instead of prunes and return the tray to the oven for a couple of minutes after adding them, to warm through.

Roast ratatouille with herbs and seeds

Making a traditional ratatouille can be a faff – finely slicing all the veg and laborious slow-cooking. I don't have the patience for this but I love the flavours of a ratatouille so this is my cheaty method, which you can have on the table in less than half the time. It's still a glorious dish. A handful of seeds adds a delightful nutty crunch.

Serves 4

1 aubergine
2 courgettes
1 red onion
6 large, ripe tomatoes, quartered
2 tbsp olive oil
500g passata
150g tomato purée
3 garlic cloves, finely chopped
A bunch of basil, leaves picked
 and torn
A bunch of dill, sprigs picked
 and roughly chopped
A small bunch of flat-leaf parsley,
 leaves picked and roughly
 chopped
A small bunch of chives,
 finely chopped
50g sunflower seeds
50g pumpkin seeds
Sea salt and freshly cracked
 black pepper

Preheat the oven to 220°C/210°C Fan/Gas 7.

Cut the aubergine, courgettes and onion into 2–3cm chunks and place in a roasting dish with the tomatoes and olive oil. Toss together, season lightly with salt and pepper and cook in the oven for 15 minutes.

In the meantime, put the passata, tomato purée, garlic and herbs into a bowl, season well with salt and pepper and whisk together.

Take the roasting dish from the oven, pour the tomato mixture over the veg, stir and return to the oven. Cook for a further 20 minutes, stirring halfway through.

Remove from the oven and scatter the sunflower and pumpkin seeds over the ratatouille. Roast for another 5 minutes until all the veg are cooked and the sauce is thickened. Serve straight from the dish.

Swaps
Squash works well in place of the aubergine, and you can vary the fresh herbs as you like – just make sure there's plenty of them.

Asparagus with spinach and roasted garlic butter

This is a lovely way to enjoy asparagus during its all-too-short season, from around the end of April until late June. This dish may be in the Sides chapter but I'll happily eat it for lunch or supper, with a slab of sourdough to mop up the delicious garlicky butter.

Serves 4

2 bunches of asparagus
200g spinach (tougher stalks removed and roughly chopped if using large leaf spinach)
A bunch of flat-leaf parsley, leaves picked and roughly chopped
1 lemon, halved
Sea salt and freshly cracked black pepper

For the roasted garlic butter
1 garlic bulb
1 tbsp extra virgin olive oil
150g unsalted butter, softened

First, prepare the garlic butter. Preheat the oven to 180°C/160°C Fan/Gas 4. Place the garlic bulb in the centre of a piece of foil large enough to wrap and enclose it. Trickle over the extra virgin olive oil and season with salt and pepper. Wrap in the foil and cook in the oven for 1 hour. Remove and allow to cool.

Put the butter into a bowl. Unwrap the garlic and cut a small slice off the bottom. Gently squeeze the garlic bulb from the top down and the soft garlic should just slip out of the papery skin. Add it to the butter, season with a little salt and pepper and mix together to combine.

Turn the oven up to 230°C/220°C Fan/Gas 8. Bend each asparagus spear until it naturally breaks – it will break at its sweet spot. (Don't discard the tougher ends, use them for soups and slow-cooked dishes.)

Lay the asparagus in a roasting tray, dot the garlic butter all over them and season with salt and pepper. Place in the oven for 3 minutes. Take out the tray and stir through the spinach and chopped parsley. Return to the oven for 2 minutes until the spinach is fully wilted, then remove.

Squeeze over the juice from the halved lemon and toss together. Taste to check the seasoning and adjust as necessary, then serve – making sure you use every scrap of the delicious butter.

Swaps
Purple sprouting, tenderstem broccoli and wedges of fennel all work nicely in place of asparagus – adjust the cooking time accordingly.

Roast tomatoes with fennel, preserved lemon and chilli

All of these ingredients marry harmoniously to make an incredible dish. I often have this as a side but it also makes a great base for fillets of white fish or small whole mackerel, or even fresh mussels, to create a fabulous main dish. I've even been known to eat it straight from the roasting tray for supper – it's that delicious.

Serves 4

2 fennel bulbs
3 tbsp extra virgin olive oil
8 large ripe tomatoes, quartered
400g tin chopped tomatoes
200g cherry tomatoes on-the-vine, stalks removed
1 medium-hot chilli, deseeded and finely chopped
½ preserved lemon, peel only, finely chopped
2 tbsp capers, roughly chopped
A small bunch of dill, sprigs picked and roughly chopped
Sea salt and freshly cracked black pepper

Preheat the oven to 220°C/210°C Fan/Gas 7.

Slice each fennel bulb vertically into 6 wedges and place the wedges in a roasting tray. Trickle over the extra virgin olive oil and season with salt and pepper. Roast in the oven for 15 minutes.

Take the tray from the oven and add all the rest of the ingredients, seasoning lightly. Stir gently, taking care to avoid breaking apart the fennel, then level the mix by carefully shaking the tray.

Return to the oven and cook for 15 minutes, or until the fennel is just tender. Serve piping hot.

Swaps
Wedges of red onion make a nice alternative to fennel.

All the alliums with sage and thyme

Alliums are the cornerstone of many dishes and they complement each other well so I thought I'd bring a load of them together. Roasting makes them beautifully sweet, and by adding them in stages you get a variety of textures and sweetness. The spring onions and chives go in at the last minute to deliver a whack of hot onion flavour. This is equally good alongside fish or meat, or you can add toasted nuts and seeds to turn it into a main event.

Serves 4

3 medium onions, quartered
3 tbsp extra virgin olive oil
2 leeks, trimmed and cut into
    2cm pieces
4 garlic cloves, roughly chopped
6 generous sprigs of thyme
A bunch of spring onions, trimmed
    and cut into 3cm pieces
A small bunch of sage, leaves
    picked and roughly chopped
A small bunch of chives,
    finely chopped
Sea salt and freshly cracked
    black pepper

Preheat the oven to 200°C/180°C Fan/Gas 6.

Put the quartered onions and extra virgin olive oil into a large roasting tray, toss together and season well with salt and pepper. Cook in the oven for 10 minutes.

Take the roasting tray from the oven and add the leeks, garlic and thyme. Stir to mix and return to the oven for 20 minutes, or until the onions and leeks have gained a little colour and are nice and soft.

Add the spring onions, sage and chives and cook in the oven for a further 5 minutes. Taste to check the seasoning, adding a little more salt and pepper if needed. Serve straight away.

Swaps
You can include fresh garlic (also known as 'wet garlic') when it's in season during late spring, omitting the ordinary garlic. Pop a few fresh garlic bulbs in with the onions – they will become deliciously soft, sweet and creamy on roasting.

Squash with red onions, olives and orange

Squash is such a wonderfully versatile veg, it goes with almost anything. This is perfect served piping hot to accompany a wintry roast or, if left to cool to room temperature, it's the basis for a lovely salad – simply scatter over a few peppery leaves and a crumble of your favourite cheese.

Serves 4

1kg squash, such as butternut or Crown Prince, peeled and deseeded
4 red onions, cut into thin wedges
3 garlic cloves, finely sliced
100g Kalamata olives, pitted
2 oranges, quartered (any obvious pips removed)
4 sprigs of thyme
6 bay leaves
2 sprigs of rosemary
3 tbsp extra virgin olive oil
Sea salt and freshly cracked black pepper

Preheat the oven to 220°C/210°C Fan/Gas 7.

Cut the squash into 2–3cm chunks and place in a roasting tray. Add all of the remaining ingredients, seasoning with some salt and plenty of black pepper. Toss together and cook in the oven for 15 minutes.

Take out the tray, give everything a good stir and then return to the oven for 10 minutes, or until the squash is tender. Depending on the squash, it may need another 5 minutes.

Remove from the oven and taste to check the seasoning, adjusting it if you need to. Carefully squeeze over the juice from 2 orange wedges in the tray (they'll be hot so be careful). Serve straight away.

Swaps
Try substituting the oranges with quartered cored apples and the olives with capers. Add the apples halfway through cooking rather than at the start, to ensure they don't break up completely.

Cabbage, carrots and shallots with hazelnut satay

Cabbage is the star of the show here. I love roasting this vegetable as it intensifies the flavour to give a wonderful nutty taste, especially if you get some good colour on the cut edges. The satay sauce is the ideal complement – I'm using hazelnut butter here, but any nut or seed butter will do. It's an excellent accompaniment to the roast chicken on page 126.

Serves 4 (generously)

450g carrots
250g shallots
3 tbsp cold-pressed rapeseed oil
1 large or 2 small pointed (hispi) cabbage(s), outer leaves removed
Sea salt and freshly cracked black pepper

For the satay
Finely grated zest and juice of 1 lime
1 tsp honey
2 tbsp tamari (or soy sauce)
2 tbsp good-quality medium-hot curry powder
3 tbsp hazelnut butter (or peanut butter)
400ml coconut milk

To finish
5 sprigs of mint, leaves picked and roughly torn
A small bunch of coriander, leaves picked and roughly chopped

Preheat the oven to 230°C/220°C Fan/Gas 8.

Cut the carrots on an angle into 2.5cm pieces and place in a roasting dish with the peeled whole shallots. Trickle over 2 tbsp of the rapeseed oil, season with salt and pepper and toss together. Roast in the oven for 20 minutes, stirring halfway through.

In the meantime, quarter the cabbage(s) lengthways and rub the cut surfaces with the remaining 1 tbsp oil. Season with salt and pepper.

Remove the dish from the oven and squidge the cabbage wedges, cut side up, in among the carrots and shallots. Return to the oven and cook for another 10 minutes.

While the veg is roasting, mix all the satay ingredients together in a bowl until smoothly combined. Season with salt and pepper to taste.

Take the dish from the oven and stir the satay through the veg, making sure it coats everything, especially the cut sides of the cabbage. Return to the oven and cook for a further 10 minutes.

Remove from the oven, taste to check the seasoning and adjust as necessary. Scatter over the herbs to serve.

Swap
Large cauliflower florets are a great alternative to the cabbage wedges; you'll need a medium cauliflower.

Carrots, honey, orange and thyme

This classic flavour combination is a perfect partner for pretty much any Sunday roast. Honey helps to achieve those sticky caramelised edges on the carrots and lends a touch of extra sweetness. To turn it into a great lunch, simply add a crumble of goat's cheese or ricotta and a crisp salad.

Serves 4

1kg carrots
2 tbsp cold-pressed rapeseed oil
2 medium oranges
5 sprigs of thyme
4–5 bay leaves
1 tbsp honey
Sea salt and freshly cracked
    black pepper

Preheat the oven to 220°C/210°C Fan/Gas 7.

Cut the carrots on an angle into 2–3cm pieces. Tip into a roasting tray, trickle over the rapeseed oil and season with salt and pepper. Roast in the oven for 15 minutes.

In the meantime, finely grate the zest from the oranges and set aside. Cut away all the white pith from the zested oranges then slice them into rounds.

Remove the tray from the oven, turn the carrots and add the orange slices, thyme sprigs, bay leaves, honey and orange zest. Return to the oven for 20 minutes. Taste to check the seasoning and adjust as necessary, then serve.

Swaps
Try using a mixture of swede, parsnips and carrots or turnips for a full array of roots.

Celeriac with raisins, almonds and parsley

Celeriac is one of my favourite vegetables and roasting it is my preferred way of cooking it – getting a nice colour on the cut edges is key. It works so well here with the sweet pop of plump soaked raisins and the crunch of almonds. If you're not familiar with celeriac, don't be put off by the way it looks. It has a great flavour, is versatile, keeps well and you can get it almost all year round.

Serves 4

1 large or 2 medium celeriac
2 medium onions
2 garlic cloves, finely sliced
4 sprigs of thyme
2 tbsp extra virgin olive oil
150g raisins, soaked overnight
  in 200ml cider or apple juice
½ preserved lemon, peel only,
  finely chopped (or grated zest
  and juice of 1 fresh lemon)
150g almonds (skin on),
  roughly chopped
A small bunch of flat-leaf parsley,
  leaves picked and roughly
  chopped
Sea salt and freshly cracked
  black pepper

Preheat the oven to 230°C/220°C Fan/Gas 8.

Cut the peeled celeriac into 2–3cm pieces and the onions into 1cm wedges. Put both veg into a roasting tray with the garlic, thyme and extra virgin olive oil. Season with salt and pepper, toss together and roast in the oven for 15 minutes, stirring halfway through.

Take the tray out of the oven and add the raisins together with any residual soaking liquor, the preserved (or fresh) lemon and almonds. Stir together and return to the oven for 5–10 minutes, or until the celeriac is just softened.

Remove from the oven and toss through the chopped parsley. Taste to check the seasoning and adjust as necessary, then serve.

Swaps
Instead of the celeriac, use wedges of fennel or big florets of cauliflower. Both work well, just adjust the cooking time accordingly.

Celeriac, apple, leek and capers

All of these ingredients are in season together and what grows together, goes together! The apples add a sweet edge to cut through the earthy, rich celeriac and the little salty hits of caper are a joy. This is a great companion to roast white fish; I also enjoy it as a hearty stand-alone supper, scattered with toasted walnuts.

Serves 4

1 large celeriac
4 leeks, trimmed
2 tbsp extra virgin olive oil
2–3 eating apples, such as
    Cox's or Gala
25g capers, roughly chopped
A small bunch of flat-leaf parsley,
    leaves picked and roughly
    chopped
Sea salt and freshly cracked
    black pepper

Preheat the oven to 220°C/210°C Fan/Gas 7.

Cut the peeled celeriac into 2–3cm chunks. Slice the leeks on an angle into 2–3cm slices. Place both veg in a roasting dish or tray. Trickle over the extra virgin olive oil, season with salt and pepper and toss to coat. Roast in the oven for 10 minutes.

Take out the roasting tray, give the veg a stir and then return to the oven for 10–15 minutes, until the celeriac is just starting to soften.

In the meantime, quarter and core the apples then cut into chunky wedges. Remove the tray from the oven, add the apple wedges and capers, stir and roast for a further 5 minutes.

Remove from the oven and stir through the chopped parsley. Taste to check the seasoning and adjust as necessary, then serve.

Swaps
Use quartered, cored pears instead of the apple wedges. You can also replace the celeriac with peeled whole Jerusalem artichokes.

Curried parsnips and pears

Parsnip and curry spices are a match made in heaven and I love cooking this earthy root with fruit too, so this is a regular feature in our house. Rich, spicy and sweet, with a lovely hit of lime juice, everything melds together beautifully.

Serves 4

4 medium parsnips
3 slightly under-ripe
    Conference pears
1 tbsp good-quality medium-hot
    curry powder
Finely grated zest and juice of
    1 lime
3 tbsp extra virgin olive oil
A small bunch of mint, leaves
    picked and torn
A small bunch of coriander,
    roughly chopped
Sea salt and freshly cracked
    black pepper

Preheat the oven to 220°C/210°C Fan/Gas 7.

Halve or quarter the parsnips; quarter and core the pears. Put them both into a roasting tray, sprinkle with the curry powder and lime zest and trickle over the extra virgin olive oil. Toss to mix and season lightly with salt and pepper. Roast in the oven for 15 minutes.

Take out the tray, give the contents a stir then return to the oven. Roast for a further 10 minutes or until the parsnips are softened, then remove from the oven.

Pile into a warmed serving dish, scatter over the herbs, sprinkle with the lime juice and toss through. Taste to check the seasoning and adjust as necessary, then serve.

Swap
Instead of parsnips, try using celeriac or swede.

Roast beetroot with blackcurrants, feta and chilli

I love introducing fruit to savoury dishes, as it lends both sweetness and acidity, and blackcurrants are ideal for this. Their season is short but plentiful so I tuck a few tubs of them in the freezer to make them last longer. (You can use them straight from frozen in this recipe.) Here salty feta combats the rich beetroot, making for a well-balanced dish.

Serves 4

5–6 medium beetroot
2 tbsp cold-pressed rapeseed oil
1 medium-hot red chilli, deseeded
   and finely chopped
150g blackcurrants
A small bunch of dill, sprigs picked
150g feta
Sea salt and freshly cracked
   black pepper

Preheat the oven to 200°C/180°C Fan/Gas 6.

Peel the beetroot, chop into 3cm pieces and tip into a roasting tray. Trickle over the rapeseed oil and season with salt and pepper. Toss together and roast in the oven for 30 minutes, or until the beetroot have started to soften, stirring halfway through.

Take out the tray, add the chilli and blackcurrants, then return to the oven for a further 5 minutes.

Remove from the oven and gently stir through most of the dill sprigs. Transfer to a warmed serving dish and crumble over the feta. Scatter over the remaining dill and serve.

Swaps

Chunks of carrots work just as well as beetroot here. You can also swap the blackcurrants with redcurrants.

Roast swede, Cheddar and spring onion mash

Swede can be a tricky vegetable to cook well and as a child I disliked it with a passion. Over the years, I've combated that hatred effectively and now enjoy the vegetable in many different guises, though I've come to the conclusion you should never boil a swede! By roasting them, you concentrate all their great flavours in this delicious mash.

Serves 4

3 medium swede
2 tbsp cold-pressed rapeseed oil
200g mature Cheddar, grated
50g butter, softened
2 bunches of spring onions,
    trimmed and cut into 1cm pieces
Sea salt and freshly cracked
    black pepper

Preheat the oven to 210°C/190°C Fan/Gas 6½.

Peel and cut the swede into 1cm cubes. Place in a roasting tray with the rapeseed oil and a good splash of water. Toss to mix and cook in the oven for 25–30 minutes until the swede has taken on some colour and is soft.

Remove from the oven and mash the swede using a potato masher (or blitz briefly with a stick blender), keeping some texture.

Add the grated cheese, butter and spring onions and stir until the cheese and butter are fully melted. Season with plenty of pepper, and salt to taste. Serve straight away.

Swaps
Parsnips, potatoes and celeriac are all excellent swaps for the swede, depending on what you are serving the mash with.

Turnips with chorizo, apples and almonds

Turnips can be variable. For the best eating experience, choose those that are the size of a golf ball (or just a little larger), as these will be peppery and sweet. As turnips get bigger they become woody and watery. Small to medium turnips carry such a good independent flavour that they can handle the whack of chorizo in this dish without getting overpowered.

Serves 4

750g small–medium turnips
   (about 12)
150g homemade 'chorizo'
   (see page 29)
3 garlic cloves (unpeeled), bashed
   but kept intact
2 tbsp sunflower or light
   rapeseed oil
2 crisp eating apples, such as
   Cox's or Gala
100g almonds (skin on), roughly
   chopped
A small bunch of dill, sprigs picked
Sea salt and freshly cracked
   black pepper

Preheat the oven to 220°C/200°C Fan/Gas 7.

Halve or quarter the turnips, depending on size, then place in a roasting dish. Roll the chorizo into small balls and add to the dish with the garlic cloves. Trickle over the oil and turn everything to coat. Cook in the oven for 20 minutes.

Meanwhile, quarter and core the apples then cut into chunky wedges. Take the dish from the oven and add the apples and almonds. Toss together and return to the oven for 10 minutes.

Remove from the oven, season with salt and pepper to taste and scatter over the dill to serve.

Swaps

Swap the chorizo out for nice big lardons of smoked streaky bacon. You can also switch out the almonds for Kalamata olives.

Three-root dauphinoise

I'm not sure I've met many people who don't like dauphinoise potatoes – it's the ultimate indulgent accompaniment to many dishes and a staple on restaurant menus. By replacing some of the spuds with a mix of roots you get a sweeter, more complex, but equally delicious end result. You can vary the roots you choose, just keep in the floury maincrop potatoes. The cheese topping isn't traditional but it does make it extra delicious.

Serves 6

2 large potatoes, such as
   Maris Piper or King Edward
1 swede
1 small or ½ medium celeriac
2 garlic cloves, finely chopped
4 sprigs of thyme, leaves picked
250ml double cream
200g mature Cheddar cheese,
   grated (optional)
Sea salt and freshly cracked
   black pepper

Preheat the oven to 180°C/160°C Fan/Gas 4.

Peel and finely slice the potatoes, swede and celeriac. Layer the slices in a roasting dish, alternating the veg and sprinkling with the garlic, thyme and salt and pepper as you go (be generous with the seasoning). Carefully pour over the cream.

Cover the creamy veg with a piece of baking paper; this will protect the cream from the heat of the oven and stop it from splitting. Cook in the oven for 45 minutes.

Remove the paper and cook for another 20–30 minutes, until all the veg are tender. To test, take the dish out of the oven and pierce the root mix in the centre right through with a knife; it shouldn't meet any resistance.

Turn the oven up to 220°C/210°C Fan/Gas 7. If using cheese, scatter it evenly over the veg.

Place the dish (with or without the cheese) on a high shelf in the oven until nicely browned. The cheese, if added, should be melted, bubbling and well coloured. Remove from the oven and serve.

Swaps
For a less indulgent dish, you can make a 'boulangère' by replacing the cream with chicken or veg stock.

Roast five-root bash

Root veg mash is often disappointing as the roots are typically boiled and become waterlogged, which dilutes the taste and nutritional value. Roasting the roots concentrates their flavour and gives them some lovely crispy brown edges, which are a joy to find as you eat. I call this a bash rather than a mash, as you're not looking to make it smooth – it's actually nice to have some texture in there. Any leftovers can be fried up for breakfast the next day and topped with a fried egg.

Serves 4

3 medium floury potatoes, such as Maris Piper or King Edward
2 carrots
½ celeriac
2 parsnips
1 swede
3 tbsp cold-pressed rapeseed oil
2 knobs of butter (or a little extra cold-pressed rapeseed oil)
3 sprigs of sage, leaves picked and finely shredded
3 sprigs of tarragon, leaves picked and finely chopped
Sea salt and freshly cracked black pepper

Preheat the oven to 210°C/190°C Fan/Gas 6½.

Peel the vegetables and cut all of them, except the swede, into 2cm pieces. Cut the swede into 1cm pieces.

Put all the chopped veg into a roasting tray. Trickle over the rapeseed oil, season with salt and pepper and toss to coat. Roast in the oven for 10 minutes.

Take out the tray, stir the veg vigorously (don't worry if they break up) and quickly return to the oven (so you don't lose heat). Cook for another 30–40 minutes until all the roots are tender enough to be 'bashed', stirring halfway through.

Remove the roasting tray from the oven. Add the butter (or extra oil) together with the herbs and use a potato masher or the back of a fork to bash the roots around. You're not looking to achieve a smooth mash, just to break each chunk down, so they meld together.

Taste to check the seasoning, adding more salt and/or pepper if needed, then serve.

Swaps
Add 2 tsp curry powder to the veg with the rapeseed oil before roasting for a spicier version.

New potatoes with harissa and chard

I always have a jar of harissa in the house: a small spoonful can take a dish up a notch, giving it a hug of chilli heat without overpowering everything. Chard, a close relation of beetroot, has a bold flavour and comes together with lovely waxy new potatoes like a dream. I'd be amazed if you have any left over, but if you do, serve it up for breakfast with some scrambled eggs.

Serves 4

1kg new potatoes (skin on), halved
2 tbsp rose harissa (or more
   or less to taste)
3 tbsp extra virgin olive oil
100g chard
A small bunch of coriander, leaves
   picked and roughly chopped
Sea salt and freshly cracked
   black pepper

Preheat the oven to 190°C/170°C Fan/Gas 5.

Put the new potatoes, harissa and extra virgin olive oil into a roasting tray, toss to coat and cook in the oven for 30 minutes.

In the meantime, separate the chard leaves from their stalks. Roughly rip the leaves and finely chop the stalks.

Take out the tray, add the chard stalks and leaves and give everything a good stir. Return to the oven for 3–4 minutes or so, until the potatoes and chard are cooked.

Add the chopped coriander and stir through. Taste to check the seasoning and adjust as necessary, then serve.

Swaps

For a different end result (without swapping ingredients) roughly mash the potatoes with a potato masher. This will take your bangers and mash to a whole new level.

New potatoes with lemon, chilli and coriander

When the first new potatoes appear in early spring, it's a sign that more abundant times are on their way, and this is a great way to honour them. It's a simple dish but the key is the lemon, which really gives it a lift.

Serves 4

1kg new potatoes (skin on), larger ones halved
1 tbsp coriander seeds, lightly bashed
1 medium-hot red chilli, finely sliced
2 tbsp extra virgin olive oil
Finely grated zest and juice of 2 lemons
Sea salt and freshly cracked black pepper

Preheat the oven to 220°C/200°C Fan/Gas 7.

Put the new potatoes into a roasting pan or tray. Using a pestle and mortar, lightly bash the coriander seeds and add to the tray with the sliced chilli, extra virgin olive oil and lemon zest. Season with some salt and pepper and toss together.

Roast in the oven for 20–25 minutes until the potatoes are tender, stirring halfway through. Remove from the oven, trickle over the lemon juice and serve.

Swaps

Use coriander leaves instead of seeds, roughly chopping a large handful and stirring them through just before serving. Later in the season mid potatoes or main crops, cut into 5cm cubes, can replace the new season spuds. You can also substitute half of the potatoes with celeriac.

7
FRUITY NUMBERS

Fruit loves to be roasted – especially British fruit varieties. The heat of the oven brings out the best of apples, pears, plums and rhubarb in particular, and it's a great way to use fruit that refuses to ripen. At River Cottage, we favour simple desserts that celebrate fruit in season, so a wintry River Cottage Sunday lunch is often rounded off with a lovely steamed pudding or fruit crumble and custard.

All of the desserts in this chapter are easy to prepare and cook in the oven. The most challenging is my Rhubarb upside-down cake (on page 233), but even that's not difficult. You don't even need a mixer – it can all be done by hand.

If you want to make your puds plant-based, swap out butter for coconut oil, and use non-dairy alternatives to milk, yoghurt, ice cream and cream. At River Cottage, we avoid soya because it is not environmentally friendly. (Most soya is grown in deforested rain forests and trees are still being felled to grow more of it.) For this reason, we use oat- and coconut-based replacements, where possible.

Naturally, I've followed the River Cottage food philosophy, keeping things simple yet looking impressive, dialling back the sugar and using healthy ingredients like whole grains, nuts and seasonal fruit. Try Roast pears with ginger and toffee (page 218), Plums with orange, chilli and chocolate (page 221), or Vanilla and thyme roasted peaches with raspberry sauce (page 227). Or for a comforting warming pudding, serve up one of the fruity crumbles on pages 229 and 237.

Apples stuffed with cinnamon, seeds and sugar

This is a favourite dessert from my childhood. Made with apples scrumped from a tiny orchard a short walk from our house, it was the ultimate early autumn pudding. Although this recipe specifies eating apples, I also make it with cooking apples as I do love their sharpness – especially when paired with a good puddle of sweet custard.

Serves 6

20g sunflower seeds
20g pumpkin seeds
6 medium eating apples
80g butter, softened
30g dark muscovado sugar
1 tsp ground cinnamon
Finely grated zest and juice of
    1 orange
Finely grated zest and juice of
    1 lime
1 tsp chia seeds
60g prunes, finely chopped
Custard (see page 233),
    pouring cream or natural
    yoghurt, to serve

Preheat the oven to 180°C/160°C Fan/Gas 4.

Scatter the sunflower and pumpkin seeds on a baking tray and toast in the oven for 8 minutes, or until just starting to take on a little colour. Remove from the oven, tip onto a plate and leave to cool.

Using an apple corer, scoop out the core from each apple. Now use a sharp knife to score a line just through the skin all around the circumference of each apple (this allows the apples to expand on roasting without bursting the skins).

Using a pestle and mortar, roughly crush the sunflower and pumpkin seeds and tip them into a small bowl. Add the butter, sugar, cinnamon, citrus zest, chia seeds and chopped prunes. Mix thoroughly, then stuff the mixture into the apple cavities.

Sit the apples in a small roasting dish in which they fit relatively snugly. Poor the citrus juice into the dish and place in the oven. Cook for 30–40 minutes or until the apples are soft when you push a skewer into the middle.

Serve the baked apples hot, with custard, pouring cream or yoghurt.

Swaps
You can swap the seeds for a combination of nuts, and the prunes for dates.

Rhubarb with star anise and orange

Rhubarb is my favourite 'fruit', not least because the appearance of the first forced rhubarb signals the end of winter. The delicate champagne-pink stalks are fantastic, but I'm equally keen on the less colourful but more flavourful outdoor rhubarb that comes into season later. You just need to adapt the way you treat this 'fruit' through the year – the rule of thumb being the later in the year the longer you'll need to cook it and the sharper it will be, so you may need extra sweetness.

Serves 4

500g trimmed rhubarb
  (about 6 stalks)
2 oranges
4 star anise
40g fresh ginger, sliced
1 sprig of rosemary
2 tbsp honey (or golden caster
  sugar for a vegan option)
100ml freshly squeezed
  orange juice
Crème fraîche, to serve

Preheat the oven to 200°C/180°C Fan/Gas 6.

Cut the rhubarb into 5cm lengths and place in a roasting tray. Finely grate the zest from the oranges and add to the tray then cut the fruit into quarters and add these too. Scatter over the star anise, ginger and rosemary. Trickle over the honey, mix together well and then pour on the orange juice.

Place in the oven and cook for 7–15 minutes, depending on the type of rhubarb. To check, squeeze a piece of rhubarb – it should just break under a little pressure. Remove from the oven and pick out the star anise and rosemary stalk.

Serve the rhubarb hot, or at room temperature or chilled, with crème fraîche, making sure you eat all of the flesh from the oranges!

Swaps
Try substituting half of the rhubarb with quartered and cored eating apples.

Roast pears with ginger and toffee

You often come across pears that are slightly hard and under-ripe. Eating these straight up isn't pleasant, but they are actually perfect for this dish. If the pears are too ripe they'll break down and you'll end up with more of a pear and toffee sauce. This is my favourite pud to cook on bonfire night as it's like grown-up toffee apples and perfectly warming after watching the fireworks in the cold.

Serves 4

4 firm pears
1 piece of preserved stem ginger,
   finely chopped
100g unsalted butter, softened
150g dark muscovado sugar
30g black treacle
3 sprigs of thyme
100g almonds (skin on),
   roughly chopped
200ml double cream
A pinch of sea salt

For the yoghurt cream
100ml double cream
100ml natural yoghurt

Preheat the oven to 180°C/160°C Fan/Gas 4.

Peel, quarter and core the pears. Spread them out in a roasting tray or dish and sprinkle over the stem ginger.

In a bowl, beat the butter, sugar and treacle together until evenly blended. Dot the mixture over and around the pears then scatter over the thyme sprigs and chopped almonds. Cook in the oven for 15 minutes, stirring gently every 5 minutes, until the butter and sugar mix is melted to form a toffee-like sauce.

Remove from the oven, add the 200ml cream with the salt and stir gently to combine with the sauce. Return to the oven for 5–10 minutes until the creamy toffee sauce is starting to bubble. Remove from the oven, give it one final stir and set aside to cool a little.

Meanwhile, for the yoghurt cream, in a bowl, whisk the cream until it forms firm peaks, then add the yoghurt and beat well for 30 seconds.

Serve the warm roasted pears with a big dollop of the yoghurt cream.

Swaps
This works beautifully with firm crisp eating apples: leave their skin on and reduce the initial cooking time by half.

Plums with orange, chilli and chocolate

The combination of chilli and chocolate is well proven but here you only need enough chilli to give the dish a spicy warmth. You'll know your chilli tolerance; mine is low, so alter as you see fit. This is a good way to use up slightly under-ripe plums – fully ripe plums are best eaten as they are!

Serves 4

8 fairly firm plums, such as Victoria
2 oranges
¼ medium-hot red chilli, or to taste, deseeded and finely sliced
150g good-quality dark chocolate drops
A pinch of sea salt
Vanilla ice cream, to serve

Preheat the oven to 180°C/160°C Fan/Gas 4.

Halve the plums, prise out the stones and place cut side up in a roasting dish. Grate the zest from the oranges over the plums.

Place the zested oranges on a board, cut a thin slice off the top and bottom and then slice off all the white pith. Now cut out the segments from between the membranes and add to the dish. When you are just left with the pithy centre of the oranges, squeeze this over the plums. Tip in any juice from the board too.

Add the sliced chilli and stir to mix. Roast in the oven for 10 minutes or until the plums are just starting to soften.

Take out the dish, scatter the chocolate over the plums and allow it to melt in the residual heat. Serve with vanilla ice cream, to balance the chilli warmth.

Swaps
This also works well with peaches, apricots or nectarines.

Roast gooseberries with strawberries, mint and yoghurt

Gooseberries are fabulous but they're often overlooked as they have a reputation for being super-sharp. Pairing them with strawberries lends all the sweetness I need here, but if you'd prefer a sweeter result you can use a dessert gooseberry variety. A lovely light summer dessert.

Serves 4

250g gooseberries (fresh or frozen), topped and tailed
2–3 tbsp golden caster sugar (or honey)
3 sprigs of mint, leaves picked and finely chopped
250g strawberries, hulled and halved

To serve
Natural yoghurt
Almond crumble topping (optional, page 229)

Preheat the oven to 200°C/180°C Fan/Gas 6.

Place the gooseberries in a roasting pan, add the sugar (or honey) and chopped mint, and toss to mix. Cook in the oven for 5–10 minutes until the skins just start to split on a few of the gooseberries.

Take out the dish, add the strawberries and gently stir through. Return to the oven for 2 minutes, then remove and allow to cool. As the fruit cools, it will release lots of delicious juices.

Serve the fruit in bowls with plenty of the juice spooned over and a generous dollop of yoghurt. A sprinkling of almond crumble will add a lovely crunch.

Swaps
Instead of the strawberries, use raspberries or redcurrants for an equally delicious result.

Roast blackberry compote with sunflower seed cream

Blackberries are the ultimate free food – you'll probably be able to find a patch growing nearby, wherever you live. They start to appear as early as mid-August and continue through to the first frost. And, as the blackberries for this compote don't cost me anything, I don't mind throwing in a glass of decent port!

Serves 4

For the blackberry compote
1kg blackberries
12 juniper berries
A glass of port
100g golden caster sugar

For the sunflower cream
100g sunflower seeds
50ml sunflower oil
1 tsp golden caster sugar
A pinch of salt

Preheat the oven to 180°C/160°C Fan/Gas 4.

For the blackberry compote, put all the ingredients into a small roasting dish, so the berries are about three deep. Cook in the oven for 15 minutes, stirring gently halfway through, until the fruit is starting to soften and the liquid is becoming syrupy.

Take the dish out of the oven then pick out and discard the juniper berries. Allow the blackberry compote to cool to room temperature.

For the sunflower cream, put the sunflower seeds into a small ovenproof dish, pour on 200ml water and cover with foil. Cook in the oven for 30 minutes, then remove.

Using a slotted spoon, transfer the sunflower seeds to a jug blender and add the sunflower oil, sugar and salt. Blitz until smooth, adding a little fresh cold water a spoonful at a time if needed to get the desired creamy consistency (the thickness of double cream). Transfer to a bowl, cover and chill.

Serve the blackberry compote warm or cold, with the chilled sunflower cream.

Swaps
For the cream, you can replace the sunflower seeds with almonds or cashews.

Vanilla and thyme roasted peaches with raspberry sauce

Deliciously sweet and juicy, peaches are the ultimate summer stone fruit. Their ripeness will determine how long they take to cook, so keep an eye on them once they are in the oven.

Serves 4

4 peaches
2 vanilla pods
3 sprigs of thyme
2 tbsp honey
150g fresh or frozen raspberries
2 tsp icing sugar
Vanilla ice cream, to serve

Preheat the oven to 230°C/220°C Fan/Gas 8.

Halve the peaches, prise out the stones and place cut side up in a roasting tray. Split the vanilla pods lengthways and scrape out the seeds with the tip of a knife, adding them to the peaches with the empty pods.

Add the thyme, 1 tbsp of the honey and 2 tbsp water to the tray and massage all the flavourings into the fruit. Turn the peach halves so they are cut side down and cook in the oven for 10 minutes.

Take out the roasting tray and turn the peach halves cut side up. Trickle the remaining 1 tbsp honey over the peaches and add the raspberries. Return to the oven and cook for a further 10 minutes until the peaches are just starting to soften and caramelise.

Remove the roasting tray from the oven and squash the raspberries with the back of a fork to make a rough sauce. Pick out the thyme stalks and vanilla pods.

Serve the roasted peaches hot, with the raspberry sauce and a scoop of vanilla ice cream.

Swaps
Apricots and plums work nicely in place of the peaches but they will cook more quickly; allow about 10 minutes in total.

Roast cherries with almond crumble

Fresh cherries are such a treat. I eat them almost every day during their relatively short season and then eagerly anticipate their appearance the following year. If you're not familiar with pink peppercorns, do give them a try. Rather than peppery heat, they lend a wonderful, fragrant aniseed flavour, which is superb with cherries.

Serves 4

1kg cherries, stalks removed
100g golden caster sugar
2 tsp pink peppercorns, lightly
   crushed (optional)
A glass of fruity red wine

For the almond crumble
80g fine plain wholemeal flour
20g plain white flour
100g ground almonds
50g almonds (skin on), roughly
   chopped
50g porridge oats
80g soft brown sugar
A pinch of salt
150g cold unsalted butter, diced

To serve
Pouring cream, crème fraîche or
   natural yoghurt

Preheat the oven to 180°C/160°C Fan/Gas 4.

First make the crumble topping. Put all the ingredients into a large bowl and rub together with your fingers until the mixture forms a crumbly mix, which clumps together in balls. Crumble these into a shallow roasting tray and cook in the oven for 30 minutes until golden and crunchy, stirring halfway through, and again 5 minutes before the end of cooking.

Meanwhile, halve and de-stone the cherries then place in a small roasting tray with the sugar, pink peppercorns if using, and the wine. Toss to mix and cook in the oven for 15 minutes, stirring halfway through.

Spoon the roast cherries into serving bowls and sprinkle over the crunchy almond crumble. Serve straight away, with anything creamy!

Swaps
Later in the summer and early autumn, blackberries work well in place of the cherries.

Fig, fennel and brandy cobbler

Figs are an opulent fruit, packed full of flavour, and when you add a little brandy to them you have a real powerhouse on your hands. Try and select figs that are just ripe – if they feel overly soft, it can be a sign that they have started to rot.

Serves 4

12 fresh figs (about 750g)
50ml Somerset cider brandy
2 tsp fennel seeds
2 tbsp dark muscovado sugar

For the cobbler topping
150g fine plain wholemeal flour
90g self-raising white flour
1 tsp baking powder
1 tsp ground cardamom
100g ground almonds
50g cold butter, diced
50g dark muscovado sugar
1 medium egg
50ml milk
50ml Somerset cider brandy
Flaked almonds, to finish (optional)

To serve
Custard (see page 233),
   pouring cream or natural
   yoghurt, to serve

Preheat the oven to 180°C/160°C Fan/Gas 4.

Cut a 2cm cross in the top of each fig, then stand the figs in a fairly small roasting tray – there should be a 2cm clearance above the figs and about 1cm in between them. Sprinkle over the cider brandy, fennel seeds and sugar and cook in the oven for 10 minutes.

Meanwhile, make the cobbler topping. Put the flours, baking powder, cardamom, ground almonds, butter and sugar into a large bowl and rub together until the mixture is the consistency of breadcrumbs. Add the egg, milk and cider brandy and mix quickly to form a dough; don't overwork as this will lead to a heavy cobbler.

Remove the roasting tray from the oven and drop the cobbler mix around the figs, leaving their tops exposed. Sprinkle over the flaked almonds, if using. Return the tray to the oven and cook for 30 minutes or until the cobbler is risen and golden and a skewer poked into one of its thicker parts comes away clean.

Serve the fig cobbler hot, with custard, cream or yoghurt.

Swaps
Replace the figs with 6 peaches, halved and de-stoned, keeping the rest of the ingredients the same.

Rhubarb upside-down cake

I love this traditional British pudding. The tangy rhubarb works so well with the mildly spiced, sweet sponge and the citrus and rhubarb juices make the pudding deliciously moist. A jug of custard to hand is pretty much essential, so I've included my foolproof custard recipe here, but you could serve it with cream or crème fraîche if you prefer.

Serves 8

500g trimmed rhubarb
  (about 6 stalks)
Finely grated zest and juice of
  2 oranges
250g unsalted butter, softened
200g soft brown sugar
4 medium eggs
180g self-raising white flour
70g self-raising wholemeal flour
2 tsp ground ginger
2 tsp ground cardamom
½ tsp ground allspice
2 tbsp runny honey, to finish

For the custard
250ml whole milk
250ml double cream
1 vanilla pod, split lengthways
  and seeds scraped out,
  or 2 tsp vanilla extract
4 medium egg yolks
75g golden caster sugar

Preheat the oven to 180°C/160°C Fan/Gas 4. Line the base of a 25 x 20cm ceramic roasting dish with baking paper.

Cut the rhubarb stalks into 5cm lengths and place in a single layer in the roasting dish with the orange zest and juice. Cook in the oven for 7–15 minutes, depending on the type of rhubarb, until it is just soft to the touch on the outside but firm in the middle.

Meanwhile, prepare the sponge mix. In a large bowl, beat the butter and brown sugar together until soft and creamy. Add the eggs, one at a time, beating vigorously until combined. Sift the flours and spices together over the mixture and fold in gently, using a large metal spoon, until just combined; do not overwork the mixture.

Remove the rhubarb from the oven. If there is a lot of juice, carefully tip some into a small container (save for adding to fruit salads or cocktails).

Carefully dollop the cake mixture evenly over the rhubarb, working quickly as the batter will start to melt as it comes into contact with the hot fruit, and smooth with the back of a hot metal spoon. Immediately place in the oven and cook for 35–45 minutes. To test, insert the tip of a knife into the centre of the sponge – it should come out clean.

Make the custard while the pudding is in the oven. Put the milk and cream into a saucepan, with the vanilla pod and seeds if using, and bring to the boil.

continued overleaf

Meanwhile, put the egg yolks, sugar, and vanilla extract if using, into a bowl and beat until smoothly combined. Discard the vanilla pod, if used, then slowly pour the boiling creamy milk onto the egg mix, whisking as you do so. Swap the whisk for a wooden spoon and stir constantly for a couple of minutes. By now, the mixture should have thickened just enough but if you'd prefer a thicker custard, return it to the pan and whisk over a low heat until it is the desired consistency. Pour into a warmed jug.

Run a sharp knife around the outside of the roasting dish to loosen the pudding and then leave it to cool down slightly, for about 15 minutes.

To turn out, hold a board over the top of the dish and very carefully flip the dish and board over. The cake should release onto the board; if not give the base of the dish a gentle tap.

If the sponge (now under the fruit) is a little soggy, slide it onto a baking tray lined with a sheet of baking paper and return to the oven for 5–10 minutes; it will firm up nicely.

To serve, trickle the honey over the top of the pudding. Cut into portions and serve hot, with the custard.

Swaps
Apples, pears or quinces all work well in place of the rhubarb. Cut each of these fruit into 6 wedges and remove the core. Cook as above.

Apple, apricot and hazelnut crumble

Who doesn't love a crumble! This staple Sunday pud graces tables up and down the country all year round. I like to roast the apples first, to get a rich flavourful compote under the crumble. It's important to use a cooking apple that isn't too sweet, and the classic Bramley is perfect in this role.

Serves 6–8

1kg Bramley or other cooking apples
250g unsulphured dried apricots, roughly chopped
100g hazelnuts, roughly chopped
1 tsp ground cardamom (optional)
80g dark muscovado sugar

For the hazelnut crumble
180g plain white flour
50g spelt flour or fine plain wholemeal flour
100g golden caster sugar
150g cold unsalted butter, diced
100g porridge oats
75g hazelnuts, roughly chopped
A pinch of salt

To serve
Vanilla ice cream or custard (see page 233)

Preheat the oven to 200°C/180°C Fan/Gas 6.

Peel, quarter and core the apples and place in a roasting dish (just big enough to hold everything). Add the dried apricots, hazelnuts, cardamom and sugar, toss to mix and cook in the oven for 15 minutes or until the apples are starting to break apart slightly.

Meanwhile, make the hazelnut crumble. Put the flours, sugar and butter into a large bowl and rub together with your fingers until the mixture is a fine breadcrumb consistency. Add the oats, chopped hazelnuts and salt and mix quickly, just until a few clumps start to form.

Sprinkle the crumble mixture evenly over the roasted fruit, being careful not to compact it down too much. Cook in the oven for 25–30 minutes until the crumble is golden brown on top and the fruit juice is bubbling up around the edge of the dish.

Serve hot, with a scoop of vanilla ice cream or custard.

Swaps
A combination of pears and prunes works well in place of the apples.

Berry and apple clafoutis

Clafoutis is a classic French batter pudding traditionally made with cherries, but I like to use a mixture of fruit to give it contrasting flavours and levels of acidity.

Serves 4

2 medium eating apples
  (about 175g)
25g butter, diced
25g caster sugar
Finely grated zest of 2 lemons
2 sprigs of thyme
200g mixed berries (fresh or
  frozen), such as raspberries,
  blackberries or loganberries

For the clafoutis batter
40g plain white flour
10g spelt flour
1 tsp ground cinnamon
A pinch of fine sea salt
25g caster sugar
2 medium free-range eggs
200ml milk

To serve
Natural yoghurt or crème fraîche

Preheat the oven to 210°C/190°C Fan/Gas 6½.

Peel, quarter and core the apples and then cut each quarter in half. Put the apples into a roasting dish, about 20 x 15cm, or an ovenproof pan, about 25cm in diameter. Add the butter, sugar, lemon zest and thyme, toss to mix and place in the oven. Roast for 15 minutes.

Meanwhile, make the clafoutis batter. Mix the flours, cinnamon, salt and sugar together in a large bowl and make a well in the centre. Lightly beat the eggs and milk together in a jug, then pour into the flour well and whisk to a smooth batter; don't overwork or you'll aerate the batter too much.

Take the dish or pan from the oven, pick out the thyme stalks and stir the apples gently. Using a pastry brush, brush some of the buttery juices up the sides of the pan. Scatter the berries evenly over the apples, then carefully pour on the batter. Cook in the oven for 35 minutes, or until the batter is puffed up and golden brown.

Remove the clafoutis from the oven and allow to cool slightly; the batter will collapse back down as it cools. This is best eaten warm or at room temperature, with a generous dollop of yoghurt or crème fraîche.

Swaps
For a more traditional French clafoutis, replace the apples and berries with pitted cherries.

Directory

We have such amazing farmers, growers and producers in the UK that we should all do our best to support them. Buying SLOW – seasonal, local, organic and wild – is one of our core values at River Cottage, so we'd love to share with you some of our favourite suppliers. Some of these are local to the farm, but I've included great options that are available nationwide, too.

Veg

Our neighbours, Ash and Kate, at the truly brilliant Trill farm, supply organic veg boxes, delivering around the Axminster and Lyme Regis areas.
www.trillfarmgarden.co.uk

Riverford Organic Farmers have been trailblazers for organic growing since 1986. They deliver organic veg boxes to your door nationwide.
www.riverford.co.uk

Abel & Cole offer a great selection of organic fruit and veg delivered to your door, as well as many more wonderful organic essentials.
www.abelandcole.co.uk

Meat

Harry and Emily run a fantastic regenerative, organic farm just 2 miles as the crow flies from River Cottage. Haye Farm supplies organic meat and lots of other organic goodies, with deliveries nationwide.
www.hayefarmdevon.co.uk

Coombe Farm Organic offers a range of superb organic meats, specialising in retired dairy beef, which is well worth a try.
www.coombefarmorganic.co.uk

Fish

Based at our local farm shop (Millers), Lyme Bay Fish Shack, run by Nigel and Corinne, offers a great array of fish caught with rod and line or static net from their own boat, as well as other boats landing in Lyme Regis. Collection only.
www.millersfarmshop.co.uk

Pesky Fish is an amazing online fishmonger, with a keen eye on sustainability, connecting the fishermen directly with the consumer. They have a daily market to buy from and the fish is delivered to your door in recyclable packaging.
www.peskyfish.co.uk

Oils

Shipped by Sail import some amazing olive oil from Portugal and it's all shipped here under sail power! You can't get olive oil with a better flavour – and story – anywhere.
www.shippedbysail.org

Organic Yorkshire rapeseed oil, produced by Mike Stringer, is a real treat. You can get it from Hodmedods while shopping for your pulses.
www.hodmedods.co.uk

Pulses and grains

Hodmedods supply all our pulses and grains – everything from lentils to quinoa – all farmed in the UK and delivered nationwide.
www.hodmedods.co.uk

Dairy

Riverford Organics supply outstanding dairy products as well as vegetables.
www.riverford.co.uk

Milk & More supply dairy products including milk in glass bottles delivered to your door just like milkmen did! They also stock lots of other essentials. Try to pick from their organic range.
www.milkandmore.co.uk

General organic suppliers

Planet organic is a great one-stop organic shop for all your staples.
www.planetorganic.com

Whole Foods Online is another excellent organic supplier, perfect for topping up your storecupboard.
www.buywholefoodsonline.co.uk

Index

Acknowledgements

This book has been such a pleasure to write and as always there is no way I can profess that it's all my own work. Simply, the subject matter drew me to family and friends' recipes and stories which I feel privileged to share and hopefully I've recreated with love, respect and ultimately success. I never want to single people out but the following all need a special mention:

Let me begin with the two most important people in my life, Hayley and Willow. I literally wrote this book sat next to you. You both know just when I need that hug! Thanks for putting up with me and being so amazing every minute of every day. I love you both. Without you, none of this would of have happened. (And let's not forget Mitten, Treacle and Lillie.)

To Hugh Fearnley-Whittingstall, for the support and guidance he gives me and everyone else at River Cottage to cook with conscience – not only for the ingredients but also for the environment. Not to mention the loan of a fair few roasting trays and casserole dishes! I've loved the first eleven years and look forward to the second.

Thanks to Gill Meller, who has helped make this book beautiful and been a great sounding board for new recipes and ways to improve them. He's one of the most talented chefs I know and it's always great to spend the day cooking together.

To photographer extraordinaire, Emma Lee, and her equally talented assistant Indy, who took even the least aesthetic dishes and made them shine. I don't want to ever shoot a book with anyone else!

To Rowan Yapp, Kitty Stogdon, Laura Brodie and the rest of the Bloomsbury team. Extra special mentions for Janet Illsley for ensuring this book reads and works as well as it does – your eye for detail is incredible! – and Will Webb for bringing it together in such a fantastic way.

Bob, aka Shabba, you're a legend. River Cottage would have collapsed years ago without you. I owe you so much but you may have to settle for a trip to the football!

To all members of the River Cottage team, past and present, who I've spent many happy hours cooking alongside. You're the real inspiration and drive behind me, and River Cottage as a whole. Special thanks to Connor Reed, Chiara Tomasoni, Rachel De Thample, Jonny Callis, Janine Shirley, Joshua Bond, Andy Tyrell, Joel Gosling, Sam Lomas, Mark McCabe, Jack Botha, Sam Goldsmith, Samantha Smith, Phillipa Dyer, Jim Davies, Mike Higgs and many more. Thank you all so much.

Stewart Dodd, together we seem to keep everything going. Without you this book, among many other things, would have never happened. I'll always value your support and advice, and your friendship, more than I'll ever tell you in words.

And finally, to the Alderson clan: Mum, Dad, Jesse, Joni and Amelle. You have shaped who I am and, although often separated by great distance, I still feel as though you're in the same room. Also, thanks for letting me steal your ideas and recipes!

River Cottage: Food to Inspire Change

From the moment River Cottage came to our TV screens, Hugh has championed a more holistic and sustainable approach to food. He wants us to know where our food comes from, and to understand the consequences of our food choices. For almost three decades now, River Cottage and Hugh have been showing us that food can inspire change – both in our lives and in the world around us.

Hugh Fearnley-Whittingstall and his partners at Keo Films created the original River Cottage television series in 1999. The shows ran on Channel 4 in the UK for the next 15 years. The series charted Hugh's culinary adventures, first as a downsizing smallholder at the original River Cottage in West Dorset, and later as he established his cookery school and events venue at the more expansive Park Farm.

River Cottage HQ is now a 90-acre property in an Area of Outstanding Natural Beauty on the Devon/Dorset border. The site was developed and designed under the guidance of architect and sustainability specialist Stewart Dodd, now Chief Executive at River Cottage. Gelf Alderson has been Hugh's chief collaborator since 2012. Hugh, Gelf and their team of chef-tutors now welcome guests from all over the world, teaching them not only how to improve their cooking techniques and artisan food skills, but also how to grow their own ingredients and source food in an ethical and sustainable way.

River Cottage HQ has won many awards, including 'Best Cookery School' in the Great British Food Awards, for the past 4 years running. The River Cottage Online Cooking Diploma was launched in 2020 and the Next Level Diploma the following year.

Guests can also stay at Park Farm's beautifully restored seventeenth-century farmhouse and feast on seasonal, local, organic and wild food at regular events in the threshing barn. The River Cottage Kitchen and Store, a restaurant sourcing ingredients from Park Farm and neighbouring organic growers, opened on the site in the spring of 2022.

Hugh and River Cottage have published more than 30 books, including the popular River Cottage Handbook series of practical manuals on artisan cooking techniques, gardening, smallholding and foraging. These books have sold over 2 million copies and won multiple awards, including the Glenfiddich Award, Guild of Food Writers Award, the André Simon Award and, in the US, the James Beard Award.

River Cottage also produces a range of ethically sourced organic products, including yoghurt, kombucha, kefir, sauerkrauts, stocks, sauces, wines, beers and ciders.

BLOOMSBURY PUBLISHING
Bloomsbury Publishing Plc
50 Bedford Square, London, WC1B 3DP, UK
29 Earlsfort Terrace, Dublin 2, Ireland

BLOOMSBURY, BLOOMSBURY PUBLISHING and the Diana logo are trademarks
of Bloomsbury Publishing Plc

First published in Great Britain 2023

A catalogue record for this book is available from the British Library

ISBN: HB: 978-1-5266-3913-4; eBook: 978-1-5266-3914-1

10 9 8 7 6 5 4 3 2 1

Project Editor: Janet Illsley
Designer: Will Webb
Photographer: Emma Lee
Food Stylists: Gelf Alderson and Gill Mellor
Indexer: Hilary Bird

Printed and bound in Turkey by Elma Basim

To find out more about our authors and books visit www.bloomsbury.com and sign
up for our newsletters